John Gilmary Shea, Cadwallader Colden

The history of the five Indian nations depending on the province of

New-York

John Gilmary Shea, Cadwallader Colden

The history of the five Indian nations depending on the province of New-York

ISBN/EAN: 9783337305871

Printed in Europe, USA, Canada, Australia, Japan

Cover: Foto ©ninafisch / pixelio.de

More available books at **www.hansebooks.com**

THE HISTORY

OF THE

FIVE INDIAN NATIONS

DEPENDING ON THE PROVINCE OF

NEW-YORK.

BY

CADWALLADER COLDEN.

Reprinted exactly from Bradford's New York edition, (1727.)

With an Introduction and Notes,

BY

JOHN GILMARY SHEA.

NEW YORK:
T. H. MORRELL, 134 FULTON STREET.
1866.

One hundred and twenty-five copies Octavo.

Thirty copies Imperial Octavo.

No.

Entered according to Act of Congress, in the year 1866, by

T. H. MORRELL,

In the Clerk's office of the District Court of the United States, for the Southern District of New York.

Press of J. M. Bradstreet & Son.

INTRODUCTION.

IT reflects little credit on New York that none of her sons have endeavored to prefent to the million readers of the State the life of Cadwallader Colden, a man whofe fcientific and philofophical mind, infuring him fame in any field of life that he might have felected, was devoted for nearly half a century to the development, interefts and government of the colony of New York. But his labors are almoft forgotten, his learned works acceffible to few, his manufcripts, though fafe in the New York Hiftorical Society, acceffible to ftill fewer, and except to antiquaries and collectors, his very exiftence almoft a myth. No public monument, no college or feminary of learning, recalls the memory of one who in electricity and other branches of natural philofophy was the valued affociate of Franklin, who correfponded with Linnæus, Gronovius and Bartram on Botany, with eminent phyficians in both hemifpheres on the fcience of medicine, with the

Earl

Earl of Macclesfield on Astronomy and Philosophy, whose reports to government stand out amid the mass of tedious official documents by the freshness, vigor and originality of their views, no less than by their scientific value as treatises.

Cadwallader Colden was the son of the Rev. Alexander Colden, minister of Dunse,* in Scotland, but was born on the 17th February, 1688, in Ireland, where his mother was temporarily on a visit. Designed by his father for his own profession, young Colden was sent to the University of Edinburgh, where he graduated in 1705; but feeling little inclination for the pulpit, he proceeded to London and began the study of medicine, yet without discontinuing the mathematical and scientific studies which had become so attractive to him. In 1710, allured by the flattering accounts of William Penn's colony in America, where mild laws, a benevolent system of polity and a fertile soil seemed to the young adventurer almost to promise a revival of the golden age, he came over to Pennsylvania, already the residence of a maternal aunt, and there practised physic with great reputation for five years.

He then revisited London, where he formed

---

* From an elegy by Geo. Robson it would seem that he died Minister at Oxname.

an acquaintance with the leading literary and fcientific men of the day, among others with Dr. Halley, who read a paper of Dr. Colden's on Animal Secretion before the Royal Society; but his vifit was apparently not devoted exclufively to the purfuits of fcience, as he at this time married Mifs Alice Chryftie, daughter of a worthy Scotch clergyman of Kelfo, and in 1716 embarked for America with her, refolved to make the colonies his permanent home.

He refumed the practice of his profeffion in Philadelphia, but having had occafion to vifit New York, in 1718, he formed the acquaintance of Governor Hunter, a man of literary accomplifhments, and one likely to appreciate the young phyfician. The Governor was, indeed, fo impreffed with his merit that he urged him to come to New York, offering him, as an inducement, the office of Surveyor-General of the Colony.

Colden naturally accepted such an advantageous offer, and removed to New York. Hunter not only fulfilled his promife, but beftowed on Colden the apparently unfuitable office of Mafter in Chancery.

The fucceffor of Hunter was Governor Burnet, a fon of the celebrated bifhop, who adopted his predeceffor's views and friends. Dr. Colden was already efteemed a man of weight

weight, a report of his in relation to an Act of the Affembly regarding the partition of lands having decided action in regard to it.* It was confequently no matter of furprife that he was, in 1722, called to a feat in the Council, a body of gentlemen felected by the Crown, and forming the upper legiflative houfe in the Colony. Colonel Schuyler, who had been removed on the recommendation of Governor Hunter, gave place to Dr. Colden. Honor was not the only gift beftowed; a more fubftantial mark of favor was a grant, in 1720, of two thoufand acres of land in what is now the town of Montgomery, Orange County, followed by another of one thoufand, which he ftyled the Manor of Coldengham. This placed him among the great landholders of the Colony.

His name appears in the journals of the Legiflative Council from May 30, 1722, to his appointment as Lieutenant-Governor, and during his term of fervice he was unremitting and zealous in his labors, adhering firmly to the royal governors, and often involved in the diffenfions that prevailed among the ruling families, whofe petty contentions ended only with the convulfion which fwept them into

---

* His memorial is in the New York Col. Documents, v. 807.

comparative

Introduction. vii

comparative obfcurity in the new order of things.

While others fought only to mimic the capital in fhow and parade, Colden went to work to ftudy the climate, geography, native inhabitants, civil and political interefts of the Colony. He was foon regarded as the beft informed man on the affairs of the neighboring French colony. By the Indians he was so efteemed that foon after his arrival he was adopted by the Mohawks of Canajoharie. He is fpoken of as better verfed than any other in the geography of the country, and his writings fhow that he was an early and careful obferver of the climate and its influence on health. It may not be impertinent to add that in 1723 he notices the unhealthinefs of the water in New York city, thus calling attention to the neceffity of introducing a water lefs conducive to difeafe.

He was one of the firft to urge the acts paffed November 19, 1720, and July, 1722, to prevent New York merchants from fupplying Canada with goods for the Indian trade, thus enabling France to control the weft and hem in the Englifh colonies. The act was ftrongly oppofed by fome New York merchants and the large houfes in England concerned in the American trade. But Colden rightly deemed that the greed of a few
unpatriotic

unpatriotic individuals should not outweigh the neceffity of fecuring to the Englifh colonies a direct trade with the Weft.

To correct errors on the point he drew up feveral valuable papers—among them, an account of the Trade of New York* and an account of the Climate of New York,† both of which Governor Burnet tranfmitted to England. There the obnoxious acts had led the London merchants, inftigated by their New York affociates, to addrefs a petition to the king, full of the moft egregious errors and falfehoods.‡ The King in Council referred it to the Lords Commiffioners for Trade and Plantations, who advifed that no directions fhould be fent to New York till the Governor had feen the petition and fent his reply.

When Governor Burnet received the ftrange petition he laid it before his Council, who appointed a committee to prepare an anfwer. The report of the committee, afcribed by Smith and others to Dr. Colden and Mr. Alexander, was a complete anfwer.§ It con-

---

* Publifhed in New York Colonial Documents, v. 685.
† Ib. 690. American Medical and Philofophical Regifter, vol. i.
‡ Smith's Hiftory of New York. London, 1757, p. 156.
§ Smith gives it in full in his Hiftory.

cluded

Introduction.

cluded with a recommendation that the petition and the committee's anfwer be printed. This was done, and the documents were iffued in 1724, accompanied with "A Memorial concerning the Furr Trade of the Province of New York," written by Dr. Colden.

Of this pamphlet, a folio printed by Bradford in 1724, I know only one copy, in the poffeffion of Hon. Henry C. Murphy.

"Papers || relating || to an Act of the Affembly || of the Province of New York.|| For encouragement of the Indian Trade, &c., and || for prohibiting the felling of Indian goods to the French, || viz.: of Canada."

It is accompanied by the map which is referred to in an advertifement in the work now given.*

Thefe papers were, as we fhall fee, fubfequently reprinted in England. They juftified the enlarged views of the Governor of New York, and of his able councillor, who faw the importance of fecuring the country fouth of the lakes to England, yet they beheld thefe ftatefmanlike views thwarted by men whom prefent gain blinded to great national interefts. The laws were maintained till 1730, when, by fome chicanery

---

* Page xvii, *verfo*.

not clearly known to them, they were repealed in England.*

To lay more completely before the public the importance of the Five Nations or Iroquois to the Colony of New York, as a barrier againſt the French and a means of controlling the Weſt, Colden drew up his remarkable Hiſtory of the Five Nations. Such a work was neceſſary when London merchants could aſſert to the King that the Five Nations lay ſo far from New York that French Indians lay between: and when they boldly declared before the Board of Trade that the Five Nations "were two or three hundred leagues diſtant from Albany, and that they could not come to trade with the Engliſh but by going down the River St. Lawrence, and from thence through a lake, which brought them within eighteen leagues of Albany."

This was before the days when a Britiſh Miniſter diſcovered that Cape Breton was an iſland, and a ſhort hiſtorical ſketch of the Iroquois or Five Nations and their relations with the French of Canada on the one hand, and New York on the other, was needed to teach King and Council, Lords of Trade and other ruling powers, that the Mohawks lived

---

* Journal of the Legiſlative Council, 591.

on the Mohawk, within a day's journey of Albany, as well as to enlighten them on the real pofition, influence and power of that confederacy.

Years after Colden alluded to the ignorance of Britifh ftatefmen, contrafting it with the extenfive information poffeffed and conftantly increafed by the French.

Doctor Colden drew up his work under thefe circumftances, with little opportunity for refearch, relying in the main on the papers of the Indian Commiffioners and the French works of de la Potherie and La Hontan. It was printed by William Bradford, in 1727, and an exact reprint is here given, following all the typographical peculiarities and ornaments of the New York firft printer, in order to give collectors an opportunity of having a fac-fimile of the firft local New York Hiftory written and printed in New York.

The firft announcement of it is not without intereft here, and I am indebted for it to George H. Moore, Efq., Librarian of the New York Hiftorical Society, whofe kindnefs has greatly facilitated an examination of the Colden papers, for which I am indebted to the Society.

The New York Gazette, No. 69, February 20th to February 27th, 1727, has:

"ADVERTISEMENT.

"ADVERTISEMENT.

"There is now in the Prefs, and will fhortly be Publifhed, *The Hiftory of the Five* Indian *Nations depending on the Province of New York*, giving an Account of their Wars both with the *Indians* and *Chriftians*, from the Firft Settling of *Canada* and New-York, as alfo of their Treaties of Peace with the feveral Governments in *North America*.

"There is alfo a MAP of the great Lakes, Rivers and Indian Countries, fhewing the Scituation of the feveral *Indian* Nations, from *Canada* to the branches of the *Miffiffippi* and the Upper Lake. Both Printed and Sold by *William Bradford* in New York."

In No. 70 of the fame paper, February 27th to March 6th, 1727, it is advertifed:

"Will fhortly be publifhed—*The Hiftory of the Five* Indian *Nations depending on the Province of New York.* Printed and Sold by *William Bradford*, in *New York.*"

In No. 71, March 6 to March 13, 1727:

"Juft Publifhed," etc., etc.

The work was reprinted in England in 1747 and 1750; and had thefe tranfatlantic editions reproduced that of Bradford, there would be little neceffity for now prefenting fo exact a reprint: but in fact the alterations and omiffions are fo numerous, that ftudents to whom thefe Englifh editions are familiar have really no idea of what the work was as originally written by Colden; and the early New York edition, although cited in the laft edition

edition of Lowndes as worth 1*s.* 6*d.*, is really so scarce that a few years since not a copy was known to be in existence, and the Hon. Henry C. Murphy having succeeded in obtaining one, long enjoyed the reputation of possessing a unique copy. Mr. George Brinley, of Hartford, Mr. T. H. Morrell, and quite recently Mr. William Menzies, noblest collector of Bradford imprints, who first began to gather the neglected issues of the Caxton of the Middle Colonies, have succeeded in obtaining copies. Others may appear, but they will be prizes, beyond the reach of ordinary students or even ordinary collectors.

It is unnecessary to give here a collation of this edition, as the reader has it before him.

The work at once attracted attention in England, and, according to Watts, in his Bibliotheca Britannica, was reprinted in London in 1730; but this edition, if it really existed, seems to have escaped recent bibliographers.

The New York edition of 1727 consisted of five hundred copies, which were soon taken up, and, in 1743, Colden wrote to a friend in London that "not one copy now for several years past can anywhere be obtained."

This friend, Mr. Peter Collinson, took a warm interest in the work, and frequently urged Dr. Colden to continue it. To these
                                                                    requests

requests the author at last yielded, and prepared a second part, bringing the history down to the Peace of Ryswick. The manuscript of the preface to this part, now preserved in the New York Historical Society, bears date March, 1742. He at the same time re-wrote the Introduction, and transmitted the manuscript by two occasions to Mr. Collinson.

In a letter dated April 9, 1742, he says: "I now send you the greatest part of the Indian History continued to the Peace of Reswick, which I presume to put under your tutelage because I may truly say, that it is owing to you that it ever had a birth, by your giving me your approbation of the First Part, and desiring it to be continued as a Work which you thought may be usefull, for I had several years laid aside all thoughts of it." Similar expressions occur in a letter written the next year.

Mr. Colden supposed that the difficulties with France would be settled by negotiation, as is evident by the concluding words of the Preface, which were printed as he wrote them when no longer applicable.

This Preface after reciting the struggle which led to the publication of the first Part, and the prosperous trade which resulted from Governor Burnet's policy, adds:

"This

Introduction. xv

"This History from New York soon went to England, and I have been informed, that a Publication, with a Continuance of that Work, would be acceptable. I have the more chearfully complied with this Notice, becaufe of the War, threatened from France, believing that a publication of this Kind may be ufeful, whether the prefent Inquietudes between the two Nations end in a War or a Treaty. The French have encouraged feveral Publications of this fort at Paris, and certainly fuch may be more ufeful in a Britifh Government, where the People have fo great a fhare in it, than it can be in a French Government, intirely directed by the Will of their Prince.

"I now continue this Hiftory to the Peace of Refwick, and if I find this acceptable, and that a farther Continuation of it be defired, I fhall, if my Life and Health be preferved, carry it down farther; but as I have too much reafon to doubt my own Ability to give that Pleafure and Satisfaction which the Publick may expect in things thus fubmitted to their View, I think its not juftifiable to trouble them with too much at once."

While Mr. Collinfon had the matter in hand in 1743, Colden wrote: "If that book could in any meafure draw the attention of the Miniftry or of the Parliament to regard the

the Intereſt of North America in reſpect to the Fur Trade, and the Incroachments which the French are daily making on our Trade and Settlements, I ſhould hope I have been of ſome uſe to my Country. For this purpoſe you may, perhaps, think it not amiſs to add by way of Appendix what I formerly wrote of the natural advantages which the Province of New York have in carrying on the Fur Trade beyond what the French of Canada have, and which was ſent to you by Mr. Alexander with ſome other printed papers."

Mr. Collinſon does not ſeem at this time to have found a publiſher. It was at firſt propoſed to print it with Middleton's Voyage to Hudſon's Bay, but the project of iſſuing that work fell through.

The war which broke out in 1744 ſeems for a time to have ſtopped all further movement in regard to it, but in 1747 Collinſon offered it to Thomas Oſborne, who undertook to get out an edition.

The following is the title and deſcription of Oſborne's edition as it appeared in 1747:

"The ‖ Hiſtory ‖ of the ‖ Five Indian Nations ‖ of ‖ Canada, ‖ Which are dependent ‖ On the Province of New-York in America, ‖ And ‖ Are the Barrier between the Engliſh and French ‖ in that Part of the World. ‖ With

With ‖ Accounts of their Religion, Manners, Customs, Laws, and Forms of ‖ Government; their several Battles and Treaties with the European Na- ‖ tions; particular Relations of their several Wars with the other Indians; ‖ and a true Account of the present State of our Trade with them. ‖ In which are shewn ‖ The great Advantage of their Trade and Alliance to the British Nation, ‖ and the Intrigues and Attempts of the French to engage them from us; ‖ a Subject nearly concerning all our American Plantations, and highly meriting the Consideration of the British Nation at this Juncture. ‖ By the Honourable Cadwallader Colden, Esq; ‖ One of his Majesty's Counsel, and Surveyor-General of New-York. ‖ To which are added, ‖ Accounts of the several other Nations of Indians in North-America, their ‖ Numbers, Strength &c. and the Treaties which have been lately ‖ made with them. A Work highly entertaining to all, and particular ‖ ly useful to the Persons who have any Trade or Concern in that Part of the World. ‖ London. ‖ Printed for T. Osborne, in Gray's-Inn. MDCCXLVII. Verso blank.

Dedication "To the Honourable ‖ General ‖ Oglethorpe" ‖ pp. iii–ix. Verso blank.

The ‖ Preface ‖ to the ‖ First Part ‖ xi–xiv. A Vocabulary &c. xv, xvi.

The

The Contents, 4 pp., without folios.
The Introduction, 1–19. Verſo blank.
The || Hiſtory || of the || Five Indian Nations || depending || on the Province of New-York.
Part I. 21–90.
Part II. Baſtard title. Verſo blank.
The Preface to the Second Part, 2 pp. (III), IV.
Part II. 91–204.
Papers || Relating to || An Act of the Aſſembly || of the || Province of New York, || for || the Encouragement of the Indian Trade &c. and || for prohibiting the ſelling of Indian Goods || to the French, viz. of Canada. || I...... VI...... Verſo blank. Pp. (1)–44. This is a reprint of the Bradford pamphlet of 1724, with an additional letter.
The || Treaty || Held with the || Indians || of the || Six Nations || at || Philadelphia, || in July 1742. Verſo blank. Pp. (45)–86.
A || Treaty, || Held at the Town of || Lancaſter, in Pennſylvania, || By the Honourable the || Lieutenant-Governor of the Province, || and the Honourable the || Commiſſioners for the Provinces || of Virginia and Maryland, || with the || Indians || of the || Six Nations || in June 1744. Verſo blank (87)–152.
A || Treaty || Between || His Excellency || The Honourable George Clinton, || Captain General

Introduction. xix

General and Governor in Chief of the || Province of New York, and the Territories || thereon depending in America, Vice- || Admiral of the fame, and Vice-Admiral of || the Red Squadron of His Majefty's Fleet. || And || The Six United Indian Nations, depending on the Province of New York. || Held at Albany, in the months of Auguft and || September 1746. Verfo blank (153)–196.

A || Collection || of || Charters || and other Public Acts || relating to the || Province of Pennfylvania, || viz. || I. The Royal Charter to William || Penn, Efq. || II. The firft Frame of Government, granted in || England in 1682. || III. Laws agreed upon in England. || IV. Certain Conditions or Conceffions. || V. The Act of Settlement made at Chefter, 1682. || VI. The fecond Frame of Government, granted 1683. || VII. The Charter of the City of Phila || delphia, granted October 25, 1701. || VIII. The new Charter of Privileges || to the Province, granted October 28, 1701. Verfo blank. Text (197)–283. Verfo advertifements. Sigs. (A)—O and B—T.

The third edition, London, 1755, has nearly the fame title:

The || Hiftory || of the || Five Indian Nations || of || Canada, || which are dependent || On the Province of New York, in America, || and || Are the Barrier between the Englifh and

French

French ‖ in that part of the World ‖ With ‖ Particular Accounts of their Religion, Manners, Cuſtoms, Laws, and ‖ Forms of Government; their Several Battles and Treaties with ‖ the European Nations; their Wars with the other Indians; and ‖ a true Account of the preſent State of our Trade with them. ‖ In which are ſhewn, ‖ The great Advantage of their Trade and Alliance to the Britiſh ‖ Nation, and the Intrigues and Attempts of the French to engage ‖ them from us; a Subject nearly concerning all our American ‖ Plantations, and highly meriting the Attention of the Britiſh ‖ Nation at this Juncture. ‖ *By the Honourable* CADWALLADER COLDEN, ESQ; *One of his Majeſty's Counſel, and Surveyor-General* ‖ *of* NEW-YORK. ‖ To which are added, Accounts of the ſeveral other Nations of *Indians* in *North-America*, their Numbers, Strength, &c. and the Treaties which have been ‖ lately made with them. ‖ IN TWO VOLUMES ‖ THE THIRD EDITION ‖ LONDON: ‖ Printed for LOCKYER DAVIS, at *Lord Bacon's Head*, in *Fleet-ſtreet;* J. Wren, in *Saliſbury-court;* and J. WARD in *Cornhill*, oppoſite the *Royal Exchange.* ‖ MDCCLV.

Title. Verſo blank.

iii–viii. Dedication " To the Honourable General Oglethorpe."

ix–xii. The Preface to the Firſt Part.

The

The Contents, 4 pp., without folios.—Map.
(1)–(20). The Introduction.
21–93. The Hiftory.
94–96. Part II. The Preface.
97–213. The Hiftory &c.
214. Title, "Papers relating," &c.
215–258. Text.
259–260. A Vocabulary.
   Sigs. A²—M.
   Volume II.
   Title. Verfo blank.
   Contents. Verfo blank.
1–44. The Treaty, &c.
45. A treaty held at the town, &c. Verfo blank.
46–116. Text.
117. Title. "A Treaty between his Excellency the Honourable George Clinton."
118–161. Text. 162. Blank.
163. Title. "A Collection of Charters," &c.
164–251. Text.
   Sigs. B—M.

This edition is fo abfolute a reprint of that of 1747 that what is faid of one will apply to the other; the division of the contents in the two volume edition being apparently the only change.

This catalogue of the various contents of the

the volume shows that the edition of 1747 contains much more than the New York edition. Besides the new Introduction, written by Colden, and his second Part, with its preface, which he transmitted to Collinson, it contains also the pamphlet suggested by Colden. The treaties with the Five Nations which follow may have been sent by Colden, as Collinson in one of his letters notes the arrival of a treaty just in season to print. But the series of papers relating to Pennsylvania were certainly never suggested by the author. Franklin on receiving a copy denounced it in a letter to Colden. He mentions this conduct of Osborne, "which," says he, "I think was not fair, but 'tis a common trick of booksellers." (Letter to Colden, October, 1747.)

If we proceed now to examine the volume in detail we are met by a series of changes, abridgments and extensions that require explanation.

The long title, with its geographical blunder, putting the Five Nations in Canada, is of course not Colden's. He certainly would not so have yielded to French claims as to bring the Canada border so near Albany. A letter of Collinson's in the Colden papers says, that Dr. Mitchell, a friend of Dr. Colden's, "assisted in drawing up the title page."

Introduction. xxiii

page." The author himself, in a letter to Collinson, suggested altering the title page so as to read: "Wherein is shown how advantageous the Friendship of these Nations is to the Settlement and Trade of the Brittish subjects all over North America, and what pains the French have taken to withdraw their affection from the English. A matter which may deserve attention at a Time when a Treaty of Peace and Commerce may be expected between Great Brittain and France." He adds: "This I propose for the benefit of the Printer, for otherwise I dislike promising Title pages."

Colden's dedication to Governor Burnet was merited and happy, but it is utterly impossible to suppose that he would address to General Oglethorpe, interested solely in the most remote of the British colonies on the coast, the same language, with trifling changes. What sense is there in the member of the Council of New York complimenting Oglethorpe on his applying his thoughts to Indian affairs, and telling him "not only the present generation will enjoy the benefit of your care, but our latest Posterity bless your Memory for that Happiness the Foundation of which was laid under your Care &c."? The few changes of "your Excellency" to "your Judgment," "Excellency's Administration" to "endeavors,"

ors," "the Governor of New York" to "every Governor in America," "your own" to "one," do not prevent the abfurdity of the whole Dedication as addreffed to Oglethorpe.

The real Dedication ends with expreffions of gratitude, which are omitted.

As to this new dedication, the Colden papers give further revelations. "The dedication," fays Collinfon, in a letter of Auguft 3d, 1747, "was made without my leave or confent, which makes me uneafie. I was out of Town and Mr. Ofbourn was in haft to publifh, and fo it happened, or elfe the pfon I fhould have chofen would have been Lord Lonfdale." Colden himfelf feems to have propofed no change in this part, and anticipated none. The changes in the title and dedication are therefore certainly not by Colden. There are alfo alterations in the Preface, Introduction and firft Part, of which fome note is here given. A manufcript book in a fubftantial pigfkin cover, preferved in the New York Hiftorical Library, contains the fecond Part from about the middle of the fourth chapter to the end, together with the Preface to the Second Part and the revifed Introduction. Thefe papers coincide with thofe in the edition of 1747; but there is no reference to alterations in the Preface
or

or work itfelf, nor do any of the letters preferved allude to any fuch modifications.

We muft therefore judge them by their intrinfic merit, and by this criterion we can only decide that they cannot be attributed to Colden.

Dr. Colden extended the Introduction, but, as will be feen by the few annexed notices of alterations, elfewhere the work was retrenched. This would not be naturally the courfe of the author, and on examination thefe retrenchments are chiefly of Indian names, fpeeches and the like. Dr. Colden would not exclude names, which gave his hiftory accuracy, exactnefs and point, nor omit the fpeeches to which he refers fo diftinctly in his preface; but we can well imagine that the London publifher, beginning with a view to economize, would propofe to reduce fpeeches, in which he could fee no remarkable beauty, or omit names which he could not pronounce.

The following are fome of the changes made:

In the Preface, p. vii, the words "and my endeavoring" to the clofe of the firft paragraph are omitted.

"And this collection" down to "will be," omitted and altered.

The firſt ſentence in the third paragraph altered.

P. viii. "I muſt confeſs" to "deſignedly," omitted.

ix. "For the Indians," altered and not improved.

"The Hiſtory of Indians," altered.

x. "Various" changed to "curious."

"this firſt Attempt of the Kind in this Country, with more than uſually favorable allowances," altered to "this firſt Attempt of this Kind, with more than uſual allowances."

"The firſt part" to the end, with the ſignature, omitted.

xi. "By the Dutch living in the Province of New York," omitted.

xii. "But the French," &c., omitted. The remark is, however, valuable as ſhowing how, while the French had begun to confound Wyandot and Teonontate, the diſtinction between the two was obſerved at New York.

In the Indian name for Lake Huron the word Quatoghe is omitted after Carmatare, making it nonſenſe.

"The Iſland," &c., note after New York omitted.

"Nadoueſſiaux—Naduiſſeks," omitted.

"Onnontio

Introduction. xxvii

"Onnontio—Yonnondio," &c., omitted.

"The Dutch of this place," &c. Note on Albany omitted.

xiii. "Under this," &c., omitted.

Wagunhas altered to "Dewagunhas," and reſt of note omitted.

The note at the foot of the vocabulary on the dialects and French and Engliſh notation, omitted.

xiv. Verbal alterations in firſt paragraph.

xv. "But it is probable" to "theirs," omitted. It is important as ſhowing early Engliſh knowledge of the mode in which the League grew up.

After "Sachems," the words "or old men," are incorrectly introduced.

After "Republick, by itſelf," ſeveral words are introduced.

xvi. "If they ſhould once," omitted, and the two following paragraphs transferred ſo as to follow the citation from De la Potherie, and a ſtatement inſerted as to the Creeks.

"As I am fond"—whole paragraph omitted, and new matter introduced, extending to ſeveral pages.

1. The opening paragraph is altered, the opening being changed, the Indian name of the League omitted: "the Dutch ſettled

settled New York," altered to "pos-
sessessed themselves of New Netherlands,
now called New York."

3, 4, 5. These pages are almost entirely
omitted, and the brief statement less
accurate than the original.

6. "Retired to the south of Cadarackui
Lake," altered to "fly to the Banks
of the Lakes." New matter is introduced into the London edition.

7. The account of Champlain's battle on
Lake Champlain is altered, much
abridged, and errors introduced. The
original has, "Mr. Champlain made
his men keep their Canoes at some distance," &c., showing that he and his
allies remained on the lake, which agrees
with Champlain, while the London edition says incorrectly "both sides went
ashoar."

10. The sentence beginning "It has been,"
entirely omitted.

11. Indian words are omitted as Sassakue, p.
11, or misspelt as Wabmache, given as
Wabmake; Yonnondio, as Yonnendio;
Utawawas, as Atawawas; Saguenay, as
Saquenay; to cite the errors that catch
the eye on one single page (29) of the
London edition. On the next page,
Ilinois becomes Hinois; p. 27, Mahi-
kanders

kanders becomes Mahikindars; p. 31, Sufquehanna becomes Sufguehana; p. 57, Odianne, Cadianne.

24. "This Expedition." This whole paragraph is entirely altered.
28. The fentence beginning "In the year 1667" is in part omitted, and the whole matter concerning La Salle on pages 28, 29 is omitted.
31. After the word "Calamity," nearly half a page is introduced in the Englifh edition.
32–35. The fpeech of Sweriffe is omitted and a brief abftract only given.
36–37. Speech omitted and fubftance only given.
40. The important claufe "Corlaer's Limits," omitted, and feveral others.
41. The names of Jehonongera and Kanohguage omitted.
43–47. Speeches given only in abftract.
58. "Let the river be fecure," &c., omitted. Affarigoa is fubftituted for My Lord, throughout.

Thefe few references will convince the reader that the original edition of Colden has no little value, and in the grave doubt that muft exift as to the extent in which Dr. Colden contributed to the alterations which appear in the London edition muft rank as vaftly fuperior to it.

For

For many of the alterations and omissions there seems no solid reason; the omission of the speeches is inconsistent with the preface, in which the author at some length defends their insertion, and we can hardly conceive it possible that he retained the apology when he had made it unnecessary.

That he should have reprinted it at the time without enlarging it from the accessible matter afforded by the publication of Charlevoix' History of New France, in 1744, and the curious work of Lafiteau, so full of matter relating to the Five Nations, is indeed surprising, as he must have been aware of the labors of Mr. Smith, and the certainty that he would use these sources.

Osborne wrote, June 12, 1747, to Dr. Colden: "If you have any thoughts of making any further Edition (addition) to the Five Nations, I should be glad to have it as soon as possible.. ..but should be glad if you would bring it as low as possible and add some of your neighboring Nations to it. General Oglethorpe has promised to give me great help for the other Indian Nations, and he was so kind as to overlook your manuscript, and approved it very much."

Colden, however, apparently never made any attempt to continue the History. He probably wrote expressing his thanks to General

General Oglethorpe, for Ofborne, June 6, 1748, fays:

"I will take care to pay your compliments to General Oglethorpe," a fort of proof that Colden was unaware of it till he received the General's thanks.*

Having thus given the hiftory of the work, and its editions, as far as known, we refume our brief fketch of the author.

After the clofe of Mr. Burnet's adminiftration, Dr. Colden removed to Coldengham, and there devoted all the leifure he could command from his official duties to his favorite ftudies, and to a correfpondence with learned men in Europe and America. Among the refults of his correfpondence was the eftablifhment of the American Philofophical Society, firft fuggefted by him. He ftudied the botany of his eftate, and finding a good bed of turf fuitable for fuel, made probably the firft New York canal to bring it to a convenient place of depofit, although the work may have had fome more important but now forgotten object.

In 1732 he drew up an important document—"The State of the Lands in the Prov-

---

* Ofborne gives an infight into the pecuniary matters of the edition, ftating that it coft him £120, and that he had fold only 300 copies, had 200 on fale, and 500 on hand.

ince of New York,* and in 1738 made, in form of a reply to certain queries of the Board of Trade, another communication on the Province and its Boundaries.†

During the adminiftration of Gov. Cofby he was not in favor, and took little part in public affairs. Although in Smith's Hiftory of New York his name appears among the Councillors who ordered the proceedings againft Zenger, the official Journal omits his name‡ for the year following October 1734.

In the fummer of 1740 he was appointed one of the Commiffioners for "marking out and fettling the Boundaries between the Province of the Maffachufetts Bay and the Colony of Rhode Ifland Eaftward,"§ for which his geographical and fcientific attainments fo well fitted him. In this and a fimilar Commiffion he prefided with fuccefs.‖

His retirement from political ftruggles was not fpent in idlenefs. Never lofing fight of his profeffion, he contributed valuable papers on the difeafes of the colony. He was one of the firft to fuggeft the cooling regi-

---

* Publifhed in O'Callaghan's Documentary Hiftory, i, 247.
† Printed in the Colonial Documents, vi, 121.
‡ Journal of the Legiflative Council, 642.
§ Col. Doc. vi, 167.
‖ Ib. 469.

men in the treatment of fevers. He publifhed a tract on the cure of cancers, another on the medical properties of the Bortanice, or Great Water Dock, and oppofed the prevalent method of treating fmall-pox.

In 1741 and the following year, New York city was defolated by a malignant fever, refembling the yellow fever, which at a later day committed fuch fearful ravages. Dr. Colden communicated to the Common Council his views on the caufes of the difeafe, which he confidered local, and fuggefted efficient means of guarding againft it. A vote of thanks attefted the appreciation fet by the city on his valuable recommendations.*

In 1742, as we have feen, he wrote the fecond part of his Hiftory of the Five Nations.

The Acta Upfalenfia, for 1743, contains his "Plantæ Coldinghamiæ in Prov. Nov. Eboracenfi fpontanæ crefcentes, quas ad methodum Linnæi fexulem obfervavit Cadwallader Colden," the great Botanic Contribution of Colonial New York, addreffed to Linnæus, and redeeming us from total inattention to that fcience in which Pennfylvania and Canada had won honors.

---

* His treatife is in the American Medical and Philofophical Regifter.

But

But the work to which he devoted the greateſt labor, and many years of his life, was "An Explication of the Firſt Cauſes of Action in Matter, and of the Cauſe of Gravitation." New York, 1745; London, 1746, 8vo, 75 pp.*

"In this work," ſays Mr. Verplanck, "far from aiming, as has been ſuppoſed, at the overthrow of the Newtonian ſyſtem, he proceeds the very ſame path with the father of the mathematical philoſophy, and endeavors merely to advance a few ſteps beyond the concluſions where Newton had pauſed. Newton had himſelf expreſsly denied that he thought gravity a power innate, inherent and eſſential to matter; and in a letter to Dr. Bently, had ſaid that gravity muſt be cauſed by an agent acting conſtantly according to certain laws." This agent, and its mode of action, it is the object of Colden's eſſay to point out, and he brings arguments to ſhow that light is that great moving power.

His treatiſe was enlarged and publiſhed at London, in 1751, under the title of "The Principles of Action on Matter," to which he added, "An Introduction to the Doctrine of Fluxions." This work was ſo rapidly

---

* The London edition was got out from an early copy, before the package ſent by Dr. Colden arrived.

Introduction.

taken up that in 1788 Buffon, having loft his copy and failing to replace it, applied to Mr. Jefferfon, who wrote to Francis Hopkinfon for the tract.

Mr. Colden alfo wrote about this time an Inquiry into the Principles of Vital Motion.

When Mr. Clinton became Governor Dr. Colden was again recalled to more active public life. The old parties had well-nigh exhaufted their ftrength; many of the former leaders had withdrawn; the moft prominent man of the day, Chief Juftice de Lancey, was connected by marriage with Dr. Colden, and all feemed to promife a ftate of harmony fuited to his taftes. But a rupture foon occurred between the Chief Juftice and the Governor, and Dr. Colden enjoyed the confidence of Mr Clinton to fuch a degree that in 1746, and the following years, he was urgently recommended for the poft of Lieutenant-Governor, firft as a deferved honor, and fubfequently as a defense againft his political enemies, headed by de Lancey.*

In the fummer of 1746 the Governor, in confequence of inftructions from the home government, proceeded to Albany to meet the Five Nations, and invited his Council to attend him, but all declined to give their

---

* N. Y. Colonial Documents, vi, 313, 377, 417.

attendance except Mr. Colden and Mr. Livingston. At Albany the Governor fell sick, and Colden met the Indian Deputies, and described himself as the next person to the Governor in the Administration. This gave offense, and when he printed the treaty with prefatory remarks, stating the fact that the Councillors had all declined to go except himself and Mr. Livingston, the Council took the matter up, and by resolution declared it an invidious reflection,* and some members made a representation to the Governor.

I have not met a copy of the original edition of this Treaty, but the pamphlet is included in the London edition of the Five Nations, of which we have given full titles.†

The action of the Council drew from Dr. Colden a labored defense of his whole course.‡

Disgusted with the petty jealousies of the men around him, he retired to Coldengham, and returned to New York only on the urgent solicitation of the Governor. Here he was brought into fresh difficulty, his advice to Mr. Clinton drawing on him the censure

---

* Journal of the Legislative Council, 958, N. Y. Col. Doc., vi, 330.

† It is given without Colden's preface in the N. Y. Colonial Documents, vi, 317.

‡ Ib. 318–340.

of

Introduction. xxxvii

of the Affembly and a violent attack from Chief Juftice de Lancey. To this he replied in a letter to the Duke of Bedford, November 22, 1748.*

In the year 1750, at the requeft of Governor Shirley he drew up the documentary evidence of the right of England to the lands claimed by the French, the conteft for which ended in the overthrow of French power in North America.

This was followed, in Auguft of the enfuing year, by an elaborate report on "The prefent ftate of Indian Affairs, with the Britifh and French colonies in North America, with fome obfervations thereon for fecuring the Fidelity of the Indians to the Crown of Great Britain and promoting Trade among them."†

In 1753 he addreffed Dr. Fothergill on an Epidemical Sore Throat that had appeared in Maffachufetts in 1735. This was publifhed in 1755, and republifhed in Carey's American Mufeum.

His more important public career now began. On the death of Lieutenant-Governor de Lancey, in 1760, Dr. Colden, as Prefident of the Council, came to New York, took

---

* N. Y. Col. Doc., vi, 469.
† Ib., vi, 738.

up

up his residence at the province house, in the fort, and administered the government. He solicited an appointment as Lieutenant-Governor, and was appointed August, 1761.* He administered the government till November, 1765, except a short period, during which General Monckton, the Governor, was in New York.

The government again devolved on him in 1769, but he was superseded the following year by Lord Dunmore. He was called for the fourth and last time in 1774 to the administration, which he held until the 25th June, 1775.

His administration of the Colony thus in a manner closed the English rule in New York. A zealous and earnest supporter of the British Crown, he met the censure of the public. At the time of the Stamp Act he met the full fury of the populace, and was burned in effigy. His life, protracted to the age of eighty-seven, closed on the 21st of September, 1776, before the great struggle had more than fairly opened, and while men were but just discussing the great act of the Continental Congress.

He died at Spring Hill, near Flushing, on Long Island, and was interred in the pri-

---

* N. Y. Col. Doc., vii, 461–2. New York Doc. History, 497.

vate

vate cemetery on the place. His wife had preceded him several years, having died at Fort George, in New York, in March, 1762, aged 72. He had several children: 1, his oldest son, Alexander, was Surveyor General of the Colony, and died in 1775; 2, his second, David, died in infancy; 3, Cadwallader D. Colden, a man of note in his day; 4, David; 5, Elizabeth, who married Oliver de Lancey; 6, Jane; 7, Alice; 8, Kate.

"Governor Colden," says Verplanck, "was a scholar of various and extensive attainments, and of a very great and unremitted ardour and application in the acquisition of knowledge. When it is considered how large a portion of his life was spent in the labors or the routine of public office, and that however great might have been his original stock of learning, he had in this country no reading public to excite him by their applause, and few literary friends to assist or to stimulate his inquiries, his zeal and success in his scientific pursuits will appear deserving of the highest admiration. A great mass of manuscripts on mathematical, botanical, metaphysical and theological learning, in addition to the works published during his life, afford ample proof of the extent and variety of his knowledge, and

and the ſtrength, the acuteneſs and the verſatility of his intellect."

Beſides the works already mentioned, and his extenſive correſpondence with Newton, Gronovius, Linnæus, Franklin, the Earl of Macklesfield and others, he wrote an Introduction to the Study of Philoſophy, a Tranſlation of the Letters of Cicero, with an Introduction, an Inquiry into the operation of Intellect among Animals, "On the Eſſential Properties of Light," "An Introduction to the Study of Phyſic," "An Inquiry into the cauſes of producing the phenomenon of metal medley ſwimming in water," and ſeveral papers on a method of ſtereotyping.

THE
HISTORY
OF THE
Five INDIAN Nations

Depending on the Province

OF

NEW-YORK

In *America*.

Printed and Sold by *William Bradford* in *New-York*, 1727.

TO

His EXCELLENCY

VVilliam Burnet, *Esq*;

Captain General and Governor in Chief of the Provinces of *New-York*, *New-Jersey*, and Territories thereon depending, in *America*, aud Vice-Admiral of the fame, *&c.*'

SIR;

THe *Indian* Affairs of this Province have appear'd to your Excellency of fuch Importance to the Wellfare of the People here, that you have carefully apply'd your Thoughts to them, in which I hope your Excellency will have fuch Succefs, that not only the prefent Generation fhall enjoy the Benefit of your Care, but our lateft Pofterity likewife may

blefs

DEDICATION.

blefs your Memory under their Happinefs, the Foundation of which may be laid under your Excellency's Adminiftration, if the People here, who's Intereft is chiefly concern'd, do on their parts fecond your Endeavours, as their Duty requires, towards fecuring the Peace and advancing the Profperity of their Country.

The following Account of the *Five Nations* will fhow what Dangerous Neighbours the *Indians* have been, what Pains a Neighbouring Colony[2] (who's Intereft is Oppofit to ours) has taken to withdraw their Affections from Us, and how dreadful the Confequences may be, if that Colony fhould fucceed in their Defigns: and therefore how much we ought to be on our Guard. If we only confider the Riches which a People, who have been and may again be our Enemies, receive from the *Indian Trade* (tho' we were under no apprehenfions from the *Indians* themfelves) it may be thought imprudent in Us to fuffer fuch People to grow Rich and Powerful, while it is in our Power to prevent it, with much lefs Charge and
Trouble

Trouble than it is in theirs to accomplish their designs.

These Considerations are sufficient to make the *Indian Affairs* deserve the most serious Thoughts of the Governor of *New-York*. But I know your Excellency's Views are not confin'd to the Interest of your own Country only.

The *Five Nations* are a poor Barbarous People, under the *darkest Ignorance*, and yet a *bright* and *noble Genius* shines thro' these *black Clouds*. None of the greatest *Roman Hero's* have discovered a greater Love to their Country, or a greater Contempt of Death than these *Barbarians* have done, when *Life* and *Liberty* came in Competition: Indeed, I think our *Indians* have out-done the *Romans* in this particular; for some of the greatest *Romans* have Murder'd themselves to avoid Shame or Torments, (*a*) Whereas our *Indians* have refused to Dye meanly with the least Pain, when they thought their

---

(*a*) This will appear by several Instances in the second Part of this History.'

Country's

Country's Honour would be at stake, by it, but gave their Bodies willingly up to the most cruel Torments of their Enemies, to shew, that the *Five Nations* consisted of Men whose Courage and Resolution could not be shaken. They sully, however, these *noble Vertues* by that cruel Passion *Revenge*, which they think not only lawful, but Honourable to exert without Mercy on their Country's Enemies, and for this only they deserve the Name of *Barbarians*.

But what have we *Christians* done to make them better? Alas! we have reason to be ashamed, that these *Infidels*, by our Conversation and Neighbourhood, are become worse than they were before they knew us. Instead of *Vertues* we have only taught them *Vices*, that they were entirely free of before that time. The narrow Views of *private Interest* have occasioned this, and will occasion *greater*, even *Publick Mischiefs*, if the Governors of the People do not, like true Patriots, exert themselves, and put a stop to these growing Evils. If these Practices be winked

winked at, inſtead of *faithful Friends* that have Manfully fought our Battles for us, the *Five Nations* will become *faithleſs Thieves* and *Robbers*, and joyn with every Enemy that can give them the hopes of *Plunder*.

If care were taken to plant in them, and cultivate that general Benevolence to Mankind, which is the true Principle of *Vertue*, it would effectually eradicate thoſe *horrid Vices* occaſioned by their *Unbounded Revenge*; and then the *Five Nations* would no longer deſerve the name of *Barbarians*, but would become a People whoſe Friendſhip might add *Honour* to the *British Nation*, tho' they be now too generally deſpiſed.

The *Greeks* & *Romans*, once as much *Barbarians* as our *Indians* now are, deified the Hero's that firſt taught them the *Vertues*, from whence the Grandeur of thoſe Renowned Nations wholly proceeded; but a good Man will feel more real Satisfaction and Pleaſure from the Senſe of having any way forwarded the *Civilizing* of *Barbarous Nations*, or of having *Multiplied* the
Number

Number of good Men, than from the fondest hopes of such *extravagant Honour.*

These Considerations, I believe, would make your Excellency think a *good History of the Five Nations* worthy of your Patronage. As to this, I only hope, that you will look on my offering the following Account, however meanly perform'd, to proceed from the Desire I have of making some Publick Profession of that Gratitude, which is so much the Duty of

SIR,

Your Most Obliged

And Most Obedient

Humble Servant,

Cadwallader Colden.

The PREFACE.

Though every one that is in the leaſt acquainted with the Affairs of *North-America*, knows of what Conſequence the *Indians*, commonly known to the people of *New-York* by the Name of the *Five Nations*, are both in Peace and War, I know of no Accounts of them Publiſhed in *Engliſh*, but what are meer Tranſlations of *French* Authors.[a] This ſeems to throw ſome Reflection on the Inhabitants of this Province, as if we wanted Curioſity to enquire into our own Affairs, and that we were willing to reſt ſatisfied with the Accounts the *French* give us of our own *Indians*, nothwithſtanding that the *French* in *Canada* are always in a different Intereſt, and ſometimes in open Hoſtility with us. This Conſideration, I hope, will juſtify my attempting to write an Hiſtory of the *Five Nations* at this time; and my endeavouring to remove that Blame with which we may be charged, perhaps will attone for many Faults which the want of Capacity may have occaſioned.

Having had the Peruſal of the Minutes of the *Commiſſioners for Indian Affairs*,[b] I have been enabled to collect many Materials for this Hiſtory, which are not to be found any where elſe: And this Collection will, at leaſt, be uſeful to any Perſon of more Capacity, who ſhall afterwards undertake this Taſk. When a Hiſtory of theſe Nations ſhall be well wrote, it will be of great uſe to all the *Britiſh Colonies* in *North-America*; for it may enable them to learn Experience at the Expence of others; and if I can contribute anything to ſo good a Purpoſe, I ſhall not think my Labour loſt.

It will be neceſſary to Excuſe two things in the following Performance, which, I am afraid, will be found fault with by thoſe that are the beſt Judges. The *Firſt* is, My

The *PREFACE*.

filling up so great part of the Work with the Adventures of small Parties, and sometimes with those of one single Man. The *Second* is, The inserting so many Speeches at length. I must confess, that I have done both these designedly.

As to the *First*, The History of *Indians* would be very lame without an Account of these Private Adventures; for their War-like Expeditions are almost always carried on by Surprizing each other, and their whole Art of War consists in managing small Parties. The whole Country being one continued Forrest, gives great Advantages to these Sculking Parties, and has obliged the *Christians* to imitate the *Indians* in this Method of making War. I believ'd likewise, that some would be curious to know the Manners and Customs of the *Indians*, in their Publick Treaties especially, who could not be saisfied without taking Notice of several minute Circumstances, and some things otherwise of no Consequence. We are fond of searching into Remote Antiquity, to know the Manners of our Earliest *Progenitors*: if I be not mistaken, the *Indians* are living Images of them.[a]

My Design in the *Second* was, That thereby the Genius of the *Indians* might better appear. An Historian may paint Mens Actions in lively Colours, or in faint Shades, as he likes best, and in both cases preserve a perfect Likeness: But it will be a difficult Task to show the Wit, and Judgment, and Art, and Simplicity, and Ignorance of the several Parties, managing a Treaty, in other Words than their own. As to my part, I thought myself uncapable of doing it, without depriving the judicious Observer of the Opportunity of discovering much of the *Indian Genius*, by my Contracting or Paraphrasing their Harrangues, and without committing often gross Mistakes. For, on these Occasions, a skilful Manager often talks Confusedly and Obscurely with design; which if an Historian should endeavour to amend, the Reader would receive the History in a false Light.

The

The PREFACE.

The Reader will find a great Difference between some of the Speeches made at *Albany*, and those taken from the *French* Authors. The first are genuine, and truly related, as delivered by the Sworn Interpreters, and where Truth only is required; a rough Stile with it, is preferable to Eloquence without it. But I must own, that *I* suspect our Interpreters may not have done Justice to the *Indian Eloquence*. For, the *Indians* having but few words, and few complex Ideas, use many Metaphors in their Discourse, which interpreted by an hesitating Tongue, may appear mean, and strike our Imagination faintly, but under the Pen of a skilful Interpreter may strongly move our Passions by their lively Images. I have heard an old *Indian Sachem* speak with much Vivacity and Elocution, so that the Speaker pleas'd and moved the Auditors with the manner of delivering his Discourse; which, however, as it came from the Interpreter, disappointed us in our Expectations. After the Speaker had employ'd a considerable time in Haranguing with much Elocution, the Interpreter often explained the whole by one single Sentence. I believe the Speaker in that time imbellished and coloured his Figures, that they might have their full force on the Imagination, while the Interpreter contented himself with the Sense, in as few words as it could be exprest.[7]

He that first writes the History of Matters which are not generally known, ought to avoid, as much as possible, to make the Evidence of the Truth depend entirely on his own Veracity and Judgment: For this reason I have often related several Transactions in the Words of the Registers. When this is once done, he that shall write afterwards need not act with so much Caution.

The History of *Indians* well wrote, would give an agreeable Amusement to many, every one might find something therein suited to his own Pallat; but even then, every Line would not please every Man; on the contrary, one will praise what another condemns, and one desires to know what another thinks not worth the Trouble of Reading: And therefore, I think, it is better to run the Risque of being sometimes Tedious, than to omit anything that may be Useful.

I have sometimes thought that the Histories wrote with all the Delicacy of a fine Romance, are like *French* Dishes, more agreeable to the Pallat than the Stomach, and less wholsom than more common and courser Dyet.

An Historian's Views must be various and extensive, and the History of different People and different Ages, requires different Rules, and often different Abilities to write it: I hope, therefore, the Reader will receive this first Attempt of the kind, in this Country, with more than usually Favourable Allowances.

The Inhabitants of *New-York* have been much more concern'd in the Transactions which followed the year 1688, than in those which preceeded that year. As it requires uncommon Courage and Resolution to engage willingly in the Wars of Cruel and Barbarous Enemies; I should be sorry to forget any that may deserve to be remembred by their Country with gratitude. The *First Part* of this History going abroad by it self, may give those that have any *Memoirs* of their Friends who have distinguished themselves, an opportunity of Communicating them, and may thereby enable the Writer hereof to do some Justice to their Merit.

They likewise that are better acquainted with the *Indian Affairs* may, perhaps, find some Mistakes in what is now Published, and may know some things which I know not, if they will be so kind as to Communicate them, I shall gladly Amend and Insert them in what is to follow.

C. C.

XI.

A short VOCABULARY *of some Words and Names used by the* French *Authors, which are not generally understood by the* English *that understand the* French *Language, and may therefore be Useful to those that intend to read the* French *Accounts, or compare them with the Accounts now Published.*[8]

Names used by the French.	The same are called by the English or Five Nations.
ABENAGUIES,	OWENAGUNGAS, or *New-England Indians*, and are sometimes called the *Eastern-Indians*.
ALGONKINS,	ADIRONDACKS,
AMIHOUIS,	DIONONDADIES or TUINUNDADEKS, a Branch or Tribe of the *Quatoghies*.
ANIEZ,	MOHAWKS, called *Maquas* by the *Dutch* living in the Province of *New-York*.
BAY des PUANS,	ENITAJICHE.
CHYGAGON,	CONERAGHIK,
CORLAER ou CORLARD,	SCHENECTADY. But the *Five Nations* generally call the Governor of *New-York* by this Name, and they often likewise comprehend under it the People of this Province.
DE-TROIT,	TEUCHSAGRONDIE,
	HURONS,

XII. *A Short* VOCABULARY.

Names used by the French	The same are called by the English *or* Five Nations
HURONS,	QUATOGHE. But the *French* now generally call those of that Nation only *Hurons*, who live at *Missilimakinack*, and who are called *Dionondadiks ronoon* by the *Five Nations*.
ILINOIS,	CHICTAGHIKS,
IROQUOIS,	The FIVE NATIONS,
LAC HURON	CANIATARE QUATOGHe or *Quatoghe Lake*.
LOUPS,	SCAKHOOK INDIANS.
MANHATTAN,	NEW-YORK. The Island on which the City stands was called *Manhattan* by the Indians, and still retains that Name with the old *Dutch* Inhabitants.
MASCOUTECS,	ODISTASTAGHEKS,
MAURIGANS,	MAHIKANDER, or *River-Indians*
MIAMIES,	TWIHTWIES.
MICHILIMAKINAK, ou MISSILIMAKINAK,	TEIADONDORAGHIE.
MISSISAKES,	ACHSISAGHEKS.
NADOUESSIAUX,	NADUISSEKS.
ONEYOUTS,	ONEYDOES.
ONNONTIO,	YONNONDIO, The Name given to the *Governor of Canada* by the *Five Nations*.
ONTARIO LAC,	CADARACKUI LAKE,
ORANGE,	ALBANY. The *Dutch* of this Province call this place *Fort Orange* to this Day, being the Name given to it by the *Hollanders* when they possessed this Country.

A Short VOCABULARY. XIII.

Names used by the French,	*The same are called by the* English *or* Five Nations
OUTAGAMIES,	Under this Name the *French* comprehend the *Quaksies* and *Scunksiks*.
OUTAWAES,	UTAWAWAS or *Wagunhas*, and sometimes *Necariages*, the *English* generally comprehend under the name *Utawawas* all the Nations living near *Missilimakiuak*.
RENARDS,	QUAKSIES,
SAUTEURS,	ESTIAGHIKS,
SHAOUONONS,	SATANAS,
TATERAS,	TODERIKS,
TERRE ROUGE,	SCUNKSIKS,
TONGORIAS,	ERIGEKS,
TSONONTOUANS.	SENNEKAS.

N B. The *Five Nations*, as they have severally a Different Dialect, use different Terminations, and the *French* generally distinguish that Sound in the *Indian Language* by (*t*) which the *English* do by (*d*) but I have neglected such small Differences.

A

XIV.

A Short VIEW
OF THE
Form of Government
OF THE
FIVE NATIONS.

IT is neceffary to know fomething of the *Form of Government* of the People whofe Hiftory one reads. A few words will ferve to give the Reader a general Notion of that of the *Five Nations*, becaufe it ftill remains under Original Simplicity, free from thofe complicated Contrivances which have become neceffary to thofe Nations where Deceit and Cunning have increafed as much as their Knowledge and Wifdom.

The *Five Nations* (as their Name denotes) confift of fo many Tribes or Nations joyn'd together by a League or Confederacy, like the *United Provinces*, without any Superiority of any one over the other. This Union has continued fo long that the *Chriftians* know nothing of the Original of it.

They are known to the *Englifh* under the
Names

A Short View, &c.

Names of *Mohawks*, *Oneydoes*, *Onnondagas*, *Cayugas* and *Sennekas*; but it is probable that this Union at first consisted only of three Nations, *viz.* the *Mohawks*, *Onnondagas* and *Sennekas*, and that the *Oneydoes* and *Cayugas* were afterwards adopted or received into this League; for the *Oneydoes* acknowledge the *Mohawks* to be their Fathers, as the *Cayugas* do the *Sennekas* to be theirs.[9]

Each of the Nations are distinguished into 3 Tribes or Families, who distinguish themselves by three different sorts of Arms or Ensigns, *viz.* the *Tortoise*, the *Bear* & the *Wolfe*. The Sachems of these Families, when they sign any Publick Papers, put the Mark or Ensign of their Family to it.[10]

Each Nation is an absolute Republick by its self, govern'd in all Publick Affairs of War and Peace by the *Sachems* or *Old Men*, whose Authority and Power is gain'd by and consists wholly in the Opinion the rest of the Nation have of their *Wisdom* and *Integrity*.[11] They never execute their Resolutions by Compulsion or Force upon any of their People. *Honour* and *Esteem* are their Principal Rewards, as *Shame* & being *Despised* are their Punishments. They have certain Customs which they observe in their Publick Affairs with other Nations, and in their Private Affairs among themselves, which it is *scandalous* for any one not to observe, and draw after them publick or private *Resentment* when they are broke.

Their *Generals* and *Captains* obtain their Authority likewise by the general Opinion of their *Courage* and *Conduct*, and loose it by a *Failure* in those *Vertues*."

Their *Great Men*, both *Sachems* and *Captains*, are generally poorer than the common People, for they affect to give away and distribute all the *Presents* or *Plunder* they get in their Treaties or War, so as to leave nothing to themselves. If they should once be suspected of *Selfishness*, they would grow mean in the opinion of their Country-men, and would consequently loose their Authority.

Their *Affairs of Great Consequence*, which concern all the Nations, are Transacted in a *General Meeting* of the *Sachems* of every Nation. These Conventions are generally held at *Onnondaga*, which is nearly in the Center of all the *Five Nations*." But they have fixed upon *Albany* to be the Place for their *Solemn Treaties* with the *English Colonies*.

The *Tuscaroras*, since the War they had with the People of *Carolina*, fled to the *Five Nations*, and are now incorporated with them, so that they now properly consist of *Six Nations* (tho' they still retain the old Name among the *English*.)" The *Tuscaroras*, since they came under the Government of *New-York*, behave themselves

Government of the 5 Nations.   XVII

felves well, and remain peaceable and quiet· By which may be feen the advantage of ufing the *Indians* well; and, I believe, if they were ftill better ufed, (as there is room enough to do it) the *Indians* would be proportionably more Ufeful to us.

As I am fond to think, that the prefent ftate of the *Indian Nations* exactly fhows the *most Ancient* and *Original Condition* of almoft every Nation; fo I believe, here we may with more certainty fee the *Original Form of all Government*, than in the *moft curious Speculations* of the *Learned*; and that the *Patriarchal*, and other *Schemes* in *Politicks* are no better than *Hypothefes* in *Philofophy*, and as prejudicial to real Knowledge.

I fhall only add the Character which Monf. *De la Poterie* gives of the *Five Nations* in his Hiftory of *North-America, viz.*

" When one talks (*fays hë*) of the *Five*
" *Nations* in *France*, they are thought, by a
" common Miftake, to be meer *Barbarians*,
" always thirfting after *Human Blood*; but
" their true Character is very different: They
" are the *Fierceft* and *moft Formidable People* in
" *North America*, and at the fame time as *Po-*
" *litick* and *Judicious* as well can be conceiv'd.
" This appears from their Management of the
" Affairs which they Tranfact, not only with
" the *French* and *Englifh*, but likewife with
" almoft all the *Indian Nations* of this vaft
" Continent.

Errata.

Pag. 3. line 18. for *of the* read *of these*.. P. 13. l. 9. f. *Naoious* r. *Nations*. P. 17. l. 19. for *Nipereriniens* r. *Nepiceriniens*, l. 25. dele *towards the*. P. 24. l. 13. dele *But*. P. 28. l. 13. for *accomparied* r. *accompanied*. P. 36. l. 11. f. *was* r. *were*. P. 74. l. ult. f. *Dedonondadik* r. *Deonondadik*. P. 80. l. 16. f. *did not, we should* r. *do not, we shall*. P. 94. l. ult. f. *Peterie* r. *Poterie*. P. 111. l. 28. f. *Prevent, Mr.* r. *prevent this, Mr.* P. 115. l. 23. f. *when* r. *then*. There are some other small Errors, which do not affect the Sense, and the Reader may easily correct.

ADVERTISEMENT.

There is now Published a M A P of the great Lakes, Rivers and *Indian* Countries mentioned in the ensuing History. Printed and Sold by *William Bradford* in *New-York*.

THE HISTORY

OF THE

Five INDIAN Nations

Depending on the Province of *NEW - YORK*.

PART I.

From the firſt Knowledge the *Chriſtians* had of the *Five Nations*, to the Time of the Happy Revolution in *Great Britain*.

CHAP. I.

The Wars of the Five Nations *with the* Adirondacks *and* Quatoghies.

THe firſt Account we have of the *Indians*, who call themſelves *Rodinunchſiouni*," now commonly known by the
Name

Name of the *Five Nations*, (and by the *French* call'd *Les Iroquois*) was from the *French*, who settled *Canada* under Mr. *Champlain*, their first Governor, in the year 1603. six years before the *Dutch* settled *New-York*. When the *French* first arrived, they found the *Adirondacks* (by the *French* called *Algonkins*) at War with the *Five Nations*, which, they tell us, was occasioned in the following manner.

(*a*) The *Adirondacks* formerly lived about one hundred Leagues above *Trois Rivieres*,[17] where now the *Utawawas* live; at that time they imploy'd themselves wholly in Hunting, and the *Five Nations* made Planting of Corn their whole business, by which means they became useful to one another, and lived in Friendship together, the *Five Nations* exchanging with the *Adirondacks* Corn for Venison. The *Adirondacks* valued themselves, and their manner of living, as more Noble than that of the *Five Nations*, and despised them for that reason.

At last the Game began to be scarce with the *Adirondacks*, they therefore desired that some of the young Men of the *Five Nations* might joyn with them, and assist them in their Hunting, which the *Five Nations* the more wil-

---

(*a*) Histoire de L' Amerique septenrionale par Mr. de Bacqueville de la Potherie, Vol. 1. Lettre 11.[18]

lingly

lingly agreed to, in hopes that thereby their People might acquire skill in Hunting.

It has been a conſtant Cuſtom among all the Nations of *Indians*, to divide themſelves into ſmall Companies while they Hunt, and to divide likewiſe the Country among their ſeveral Parties, each having a ſpace of 3 or four Miles Square alloted them, in which none of the others muſt pretend to Hunt; and if any Nation ſhould encroach upon the Limits of another, in their hunting, they certainly draw a War upon themſelves.

At this time the *Adirondacks* were obliged to ſpread themſelves far, becauſe of the ſcarcity of the Game, and each Party took ſome of the *Five Nations* along with them, who being leſs expert than the *Adirondacks*, perform'd moſt of the Drudgery in their March. One of the Parties, which conſiſted of ſix *Adirondacks*, and as many of the *Five Nations*, marched further than any of the reſt, in hopes of the better Sport: They had, for a long time bad luck, ſo as to be obliged to live upon the Bark of Trees, and ſome Roots, which thoſe of the *Five Nations* ſcraped out of the ground, from under the Snow. This extremity obliged the *Adirondacks* to part from thoſe of the *Five Nations*, each making a ſeperate Company; and after they had agreed on a Day to return to a Cabbin where both of them left their Baggage, each took his Quarter to hunt in: The *Adirondacks* were unlucky, and return'd first to the Cabbin, where not finding those of the *Five Nations*, they did not doubt of their being dead of Hunger; but these young Men of the *Five Nations* were become dextrous with their Bows, and very cuning in approaching and surprizing their Game, which was chiefly owing to their being more patient and able to bear Fatigues and Hardships than the *Adirondacks* were, accordingly they soon arrived loaded with the flesh of Wild Cows. The *Adirondacks* could not believe that they were capable of such an Expedition, without being assisted by some of their Nation. However, the *Adirondacks* received them with pleasant Countenances, and congratulated them on their Success. Those of the *Five Nations* made the other a Present of the best of their Venison: They eat together with much Civility, on both sides: But the *Adirondacks* becoming Jealous of this Success, conspired together, and in the Night time murdered all the six Men of the *Five Nations*, while they slept. Next Morning the *Adirondacks* follow'd their Foot-steps, by which they had return'd to the Cabbin, and found the place where they had hunted, and much Venison which they had killed, which the *Adirondacks* dryed, and carried home along with them.

The

The rest of the *Five Nations* enquired after their Companions; The *Adirondacks* answered very cooly, that they parted soon after they had left home, and they knew not what was become of them. But the People of the *Five Nations* being impatient to know something certain of their Companions, sent out several Parties in quest of them: They followed the Foot-steps of those Hunters, and found the six Dead Bodies, which the wild Beasts had dug up; and upon examination found they had been Murdered. They made many Complaints to the Chiefs of the *Adirondacks*, of the Inhumanity of this Murder, who contented themselves with blaming the Murderers, and ordering them to make some small Presents to the Relations of the murdered Persons, without being apprehensive of the Resentment of the *Five Nations*; for they look'd upon them as men not capable of taking any Revenge.

Those of the *Five Nations* smother'd their Anger, and not being willing to trust themselves any longer with the *Adirondacks*, they returned home to their own People, who then lived near *Montreal* on the Banks of *St. Lawrence River*. They gave an account of this Assassination to their Nation, who upon hearing it conceiv'd a vast Indignation against the *Adirondacks*, who being advised of the secret movements of the *Five Nations*, Resolv'd to oblige them to submit

to

to their Law, by force of Arms. The *Five Nations* apprehending their Power, retired to the Southward of *Cadarackui Lake*,[10] where they now live, and defended themselves at first but faintly against the Vigorous Attacks of the *Adirondacks*. But afterwards becoming more expert, and more used to War, they not only made a brave Defence, but likewise made themselves Masters of the great Lakes, and chased the *Shawanons* from thence.

While the two Nations were at War, the *French* arrived and settled in *Canada*, and the *Five Nations* having forced the *Adirondacks* to leave their own Country and retire towards *Quebeck*, the *French* thought themselves obliged to assist their New Allies, the *Adirondacks*, without examining into the Reasons of the War.

Thus began a War and Hatred between the *French* and the *Five Nations*, which cost the *French* much Blood, and more than once had like to have occasioned the entire Destruction of their Colony. The War had driven the *Adirondacks* to *Quebec*, and the desire of Trading with the *French*, had drawn likewise all their Allies that way, who agreed with them joyntly, to make War against the *Five Nations*, and to attack them in their *own Country*.

Mr. *Champlain* desiring to give his Allies Proof of his Love, and the Valour of the
French

French Nation, put himself at the Head of a Body of *Adirondacks*, and passed with them into *Corlars Lake*, which from this time the *French* have called by Mr. *Champlain*'s name."

They had not long been in the Lake before they discover'd a Body of the *Five Nations* going to War. As soon as they saw each other, Shouts and Crys began on both Sides. Mr. *Champlain* made his men keep their Canoes at some distance; The *Five Nations* in the mean time landed, and began to intrench themselves, by cutting down the Trees round them; The *Adirondacks* stopt their Canoes near the Enemy, & sent to offer them Battel, who answer'd, *That they must stay till Morning, when both sides would have the Advantage of the Day Light*: The night passed in Dancing and War Songs, mixed with a thousand Reproaches against each other. Mr. *Champlain* had put some *French* in each Canoe, and order'd them not to show themselves, that their appearance might be the greater surprize to the Enemy, in the time of the Battel. As soon as day light appeared, the *Adirondacks* landed, in order of Battel, & the *Five Nations* to the Number of 200 Men marched out of their Intrenchments, and put themselves in order, with three Captains in the Front, having large Plumes of Feathers on their Heads, and then advanced with a grave Air and slow Pace. The *Adirondacks* gave a great Shout and open'd

to

to the Right and Left, to give room for Mr. *Champlain* and the *French* to advance: This new Sight furprized the Enemy, and made them halt, to confider it, upon which the *French* firing, the three Captains were killed: This more furpriz'd the *Five Nations*; for they knew that their Captains had a kind of Cuirafs made of pieces of Wood join'd together, that was Proof againft Arrows, and they could not perceive in what manner the Wound was given, by which they fell fo fuddenly. Then the *Adirondacks* gave a terrible Shout, and attacked the Enemy, who received them bravely, but a fecond Volley from the *French*, put them into fuch Confufion (having never before feen fire Arms) that they immediately fled. The *Adirondacks* took twelve Prifoners, and as the Cuftom of the Indians is, burnt one of them alive, with great Cruelty; His Torment had continued much longer than it did, if Mr. *Champlain* had not in Compaffion & abhorrence of fuch Barbarity, Shot the poor Wreth thro' the Head."

The *Adirondacks* having their Numbers thus very much encreafed, and their fire Arms giving them new Confidence, propofed nothing lefs to themfelves, than the entire Deftruction of the *Five Nations*, by open Force; And upon this their Young Warriors became Fierce and Infolent, and could not be kept
under

under any Difcipline, Order or Subjection to their Chiefs or Captains, but upon all Occafions rafhly attacked the Enemy, who were oblig'd to keep themfelves upon the Defenfive, and to make up what they wanted in Force, by Stratagems, and a skillful management of the War. The Young Men of the *Five Nations* foon perceived the Advantages they gain'd by this Conduct, and every day grew more fubmiffive to their Captains, and diligent in executing any Enterprize, while the *Adirondacks* confiding in their Numbers and their fire Arms, thought of nothing but of Conquering by meer Force.

The *Five Nations* fent out fmall Parties only, who meeting with great Numbers of the *Adirondacks*, retired before them, with feeming Fear and Terror, while the *Adirondacks* purfued them with Fury, and without thought, till they were cunningly drawn into Ambufcades, where moft of their men were kill'd or taken Prifoners, with little or no lofs to the *Five Nations*.

By thefe means and their being frequently furprized by the *Five Nations*, while they remain'd confident in their Number, the *Adirondacks* wafted away, and their boldeft Soldiers were almoft entirely deftroyed, while the Number of the *Five Nations* rather encreafed
by

B

by the addition of the Prisoners which they took from the *Shawanons.*

It has been a constant Maxim with the *Five Nations,* to save the Children and Young Men of the People they Conquer, to adopt them into their own Nation, and to educate them as their own Children, without Distinction; These young People soon forget their own Country and Nation, ; and by this Policy the *Five Nations* make up the Losses which their Nation suffers by the People they loose in War. The wisest and best Soldiers of the *Adirondacks* when it was too late, discovered that they must imitate and learn the Art of War from those Enemies, that they at first Despised. Now five of their Chief Captains endeavour to perform by themselves singly, with Art and by Stratagem, what they could not perform by Force at the Head of their Armies; but they having no longer any hopes of Conquering their Enemies, their thoughts were only set on Revenge."

The *Five Nations* had taken one of the chief Captains of the *Adirondacks,* and had burnt him alive. This gave *Piskaret,* who was the chief Captain of the *Adirondacks* so deep a Resentment, that the Difficulty or Danger of the most desperate Attempt made no Impression upon his Spirit, where he had the hope of Revenge.

I shall give the Particulars of this from the *French* Accounts; for by it the nature of the *Indians*, and the manner of their making War, may be more eafily underftood.

Piskaret, with four other Captains, fet out from *Trois Rivieres* in one Canoe, each being provided with three Fuzees. In two Days they reach'd *Sorel River*, where they perceiv'd five Canoes of the *Five Nations* with ten Men in each. At firft thofe of the *Five Nations* believed that this Canoe was the van of fome confiderable Party, and therefore went from it with all the force of their Paddles. When they faw that after a confiderable time, no others followed, they returned, and as foon as they came within call, they raifed their War-Shout, which they call *Saſſakue*, and bid *Piskaret* and his Fellows Surrender. He anfwered, That he was their Prifoner, and that he could no longer furvive the Captain they had burnt; but that he might not be accufed of furrendering Cowardly, he bid them advance to the middle of the River which they did, with furprizing Swiftnefs. *Piskaret* had before hand loaded all his Arms with two Bullets each, which he joyn'd together with a fmall Wire ten Inches in length with defign to tear the Canoes in pieces (which it could not fail to do, they being made only of Birch Bark) and gave his Companions Direction

ction, each to chuse a Canoe, and level his shot between Wind and Water

As the Canoes approached, he made as if he had design'd to escape; and to prevent him, those of the *Five Nations* seperated from each other with too much Precipitation, and Surrounded him. The *Adirondacks*, the better to amuse the Enemy, sung their Death Song, as ready to surrender themselves, when every one suddenly took his Piece and fired upon the Canoes, which they Reiterated three times, with the Arms that lay ready. Those of the *Five Nations* were extreamly surpriz'd; for Fire Arms were still terrible to them, and they tumbled out of their Canoes, which immediately sunk. The *Adirondacks* knock't them all on the head in the Water, except some of the chiefs that they made Prisoners, who's Fate was as cruel as that of the *Adirondack* Captain, who had been burnt alive.

Piskaret was so far from having his Revenge glutted with this Slaughter, and the cruel Torments with which he made his Prisoners dye, that it seem'd rather to give a keener edge to it; for he soon after attempted another enterprize in which the boldest of his Country-men durst not accompany him.

He was well acquainted with the Country of the *Five Nations*, he set out alone about the time that the Snow began to melt, with the
precaution

precaution of putting the hinder part of his Snow Shoes forward, that if any fhould happen upon his foot-fteps, they might think that he was gone the contrary way; and for further fecurity went along a Ridge, where the Snow was melted, and where his foot-fteps could not be difcovered, but in a few places. When he found himfelf near one of the Villages of the *Five Naoious* he hid himfelf in a hollow Tree: In the Night he found out a Place nearer at hand, and more proper to retire into, for the execution of any Enterprize. He found four Piles of Wood ftanding clofe together, which the *Indians* had provided againft the Winter and their bufie times, in the middle of which was a hollow place, in which he thought he could fafely hide. The whole Village was faft afleep when he enter'd a Cabbin, kill'd four Perfons and took off their Scalps, being all that were in the Houfe, and then return'd quietly into his Hole. In the Morning the whole Village was in an Alarm, as foon as the Murder was difcovered, and the young Men made all poffible hafte to follow the *Murderer*. They difcover'd *Piskarets* foot-fteps, which appear'd to them to be the foot-fteps of fome Perfon that fled; this encourag'd them in their Purfuit: Sometimes they loft the Tract, and fometimes found it again, till at laft they entirely loft it, where the Snow was melted, and
they

they were forced to return, after much useless fatigue. *Piskaret* quiet in the midst of his Enemies waited with impatience for the Night. As soon as he saw that it was time to act (*viz.* in the first part of the night, when the *Indians* are observed to sleep very fast) he enter'd into another Cabbin, where he kill'd every Person in it, & immediately retir'd into his Wood-pile. In the morning there was a greater Outcry than before, nothing was seen but Wailing, Tears, and a general Consternation. Every one runs in quest of the Murderer, but no Tract to be seen besides the Tract which they saw the day before. They search'd the Woods, Swamps and Clifts of the Rocks, but no Murderer to be found. They began to suspect *Piskaret*, who's Boldness and Cunning was too well known to them. They agreed that two men next night should watch in every Cabbin. All day long he was contriving some new *Stratagem*, he bundles up his Scalps, and in the night he slips out of his lurking place, He approaches one of the Cabbins as quietly as possible and peeps thro' a hole to see what could be done, there he perceived Guards on the Watch, he went to another, where he found the same care. When he discover'd that they were everywhere upon their Guard he resolved to strike his last blow, and opened a Door, where he found a Centinel nodding with his Pipe in his mouth,

Piskaret

Piskaret split his Scull with his Hatchet, but had not time to take his Scalp, for another man who watched at the other end of the Cabbin, raised the cry, and *Piskaret* fled. The whole Village immediately was in an Uproar, while he got off as fast as he could; Many pursued him, but as he was so swift as to run down the Wild Cows and the Deer, the pursuit gave him no great uneasiness; When he pereeived they came near him, he would Halloe to them, to quicken their pace, then spring from them like a Buck. When he gain'd any distance he would loiter till they came near, then halloe, and fly. Thus he continued all day, with design to tire them out, with the hopes of over-taking him.

As they pursued only a single Man, five or six only of the Nimblest young Men continued the Chace, till being tired they were forced to rest in the Night, which when *Piskaret* observed, he hid himself near them in a hollow Tree. They had not time to take Victuals with them, and being wearied & hungry, and not apprehending any Attack from a single Person that fled, they all soon fell a sleep. *Piskaret* obferv'd them, fell upon them, kill'd them all, and carried away their (*b*) Scalps."

Thefe

(*b*) Thefe are the Trophies of Victory which all the *Indian Nations* carry home with them, if they have time

to

These Stories may seem incredible to many, but will not appear to be Improbable to those who know how extreamly Revengeful the *Indians* naturally are: That they every day undertake the greatest Fatigues, the longest Journeys, and the greatest Dangers, to gratifie that Devouring Passion, which seems to gnaw their Souls, and gives them no ease till it is satisfied. All Barbarous Nations have been observed to be Revengful and Cruel, the certain Consequences of an unbounded Revenge, as the Curbing of these Passions is the happy Effect of being Civilized.

The *Five Nations* are so much delighted with Stratagems in War, that no Superiority of their Force makes them neglect them. They amused therefore the *Adirondacks* and their Allies, the *Quatoghies*, (called by the *French*, *Hurons*) by sending to the *French*, and desiring Peace. The *French* desired them to receive some Priests among them, in hopes that these prudent Fathers would by some Art reconcile them to the *French*, and engage their Affections. The *Five Nations* accepted the Offer, and some Jesuits went along with them. But after

---

to flea the Scalp from the Skull of their Enemies, when they have killed them; and sometimes they are so cruel as to flea the Scalp off, without killing them, or otherwise wounding them, but leave them in this miserable Condition with their Skull bare.

Part I. *Indian Nations.* 17

after they had the Jefuits in their Power, they ufed them only as Hoftages, and by that means obliged the *French* to be Neuter, while they prepared to Attack the *Adirondacks* and *Quatoghies*, and accordingly entirely destroy'd the *Quatoghies* in a Battel fought within two Leagues of *Quebeck*, while the *French* durft not give their Allies any affiftance."

Indeed the *French* Author fays, That if the *Five Nations* had known the weaknefs of the *French* at that time, they might eafily have deftroyed that Colony."

The Defeat of the *Quatoghies* ftruck Terror into all the Allies of the *Adirondacks*, who were at that time very Numerous, becaufe of the benefit of the *French* Trade, which they had by their means; for before that time the *Indians* had not any Iron Tool among them.

The *Nipeceriniens*, who then lived on the Banks of *St. Laurence River*, fled to the Northward, in hopes that the extream Coldnefs of the Climate, and a barren Soil, would free them from the fear they had of the *Five Nations*." The remainder of the *Quatoghies* fled with the *Utawawas* towards the Southwestward, and for their greater Security fettled in an Ifland, which the *French* ftill call by their Name, which being further than the Name of the *Five Nations* had at that time
C reached,

reached, they thought themselves secure by the Distance of the Place."

This Expedition having succeeded so well, the *Five Nations* gave out, that they intended next Winter to visit *Yonnondio* (the name they give to the Governor of *Canada*.) These visits are always made with much Show. They gather'd together 1000 or 1200 Men, and passing over *Corlaers Lake*, they fell in with *Nicolet River*, where it falls into the South side of *Lake St. Pierre*, in *St. Laurence River*, eight Leagues above *Trois Rivieres*; Six Scouts marched three Leagues before the Army, who met with *Piskaret*, as he return'd from Hunting, loaded with the Tongues of wild Cows. As they came near him, they sang their Song of Peace, and *Piskaret* taking them for Ambassadors, stopt, and sung his. It is probable that he having glutted his private Revenge, and his Nation having been long harassed with a Cruel War, he too greedily swallow'd the Bait: Peace being what he and all his Nation earnestly desir'd. He invited them therefore to go along with him to his Village, which was but two or three Leagues further: and as he went, he told them, that the *Adirondacks* were divided into two Bodies, one of which hunted on the North side of *St. Laurence River*

River at *Wabmache*, three Leagues above *Trois Rivieres*, and the other at *Nicolet*. One of the Scouts had on purpofe ftaid behind, this Man followed *Piskaret*, and coming up behind him, knockt him on the Head with his Hatchet. Then they all returned to their Army with *Piskaret's* Head.²⁸ The *Five Nations* immediately divided likewife into two Bodies, they furprized the *Adirondacks*, and cut them in pieces.

Thus the moft War-like and Polite Nation of all the *Indians* in *North-America* was almoft entirely Deftroy'd by a People they at firft defpifed, and by a War which their Pride and Injuftice brought upon them. *Immorality* has ever ruin'd the Nations where it abounded, whether they were Civilized or Barbarians, as Juftice and ftrict Discipline has made others Flourifh and grow Powerful.

A very few *Adirondacks* now remain in fome Villages near *Quebeck*,²⁹ who ftill wafte away and decay, by their drinking Strong Waters, tho' when the *French* firft fettled *Quebeck*, 1500 Men of them lived between that and *Silleri*, which are only a League diftant,³⁰ befides thofe that lived at *Saguenay*, *Trois Rivieres*, and fome other places. After this Battle the *Adirondacks* have never been confidered as of any confequence, either in Peace or War.

The *Quatoghies* and *Utawawas* foon began to be in want of the *European* Commodities, and their defire to make themfelves confiderable among their new Friends, fet them upon attempting to return to trade at *Quebeck*, by which means the place of their retreat was difcovered to the *Five Nations*, who not having their Revenge fatiated, fo long as any of that Nation remain'd, refolved at all hazards to march through thefe vaft unknown Deferts, to fatisfy their cruel Paffion. The *Quatoghies* had the good Fortune to difcover them time enough to make their Efcape, and fled to the *Putewatemies*, who liv'd a days Journey further, where they and all the Neighbouring Nations fecur'd themfelves in a large Fort. The *Five Nations* followed, but being in want of Provifions, they could not attempt a Siege, and therefore propos'd a Treaty to the *Putewatemies*, which was accepted. The *Putewatemies* agreed to a League of Friendfhip, in which they acknowledged the *Five Nations* to be the Mafter of all the Nations round them, applauded their Valour, and promifed to fupply them with Provifions, but would not truft themfelves out of their Fort. The *Putewatemies* accordingly fent them out a fupply of Provifions, but with defign to effect, by Treachery, what they durft not attempt

by

by Force; for they Poifon'd all the Provifions. This was difcover'd to them by an old *Quatoghie*, who had a Son Prifoner among the *Five Nations*. His affection for his Son overcame his hatred to his Country's Enemies. This Treachery enraged the *Five Nations* againft the *Putewatemies*, and the Neighbouring Nations, but Famine obliged them to return at this time, and to feperate their Army into Parties, the better to provide for their Subfiftence by Hunting. One of thefe Parties fell in with a Village of the *Chichtaghicks* (call'd by the *French, Ilinois*) and furpriz'd the old Men, Women and Children, when the young Men were abroad Hunting, but they upon their return gather'd all the reft of the Villages, purfued the party of the *Five Nations*, and recover'd the Prifoners."

This was the firft time that the *Five Nations* had appear'd in thofe Parts, but their Name was become fo Terrible, that the *Chicktaghicks*, notwithftanding of this Advantage, left their Country, and fled to the Nations that lived Weftward, till the general Peace was fettled by the *French*, and then they return'd to their own Country.

CHAP.

CHAP. II.

Their Wars and Treaties of Peace with the French, *from* 1665. *to* 1683. *and their Affairs with* New-York *in that Time.*

IN *June*, 1665, Monſ. *de Traſi* being Appointed Vice-Roy of *America*, arrived at *Quebeck*, after he had viſited all the Iſlands in the *Weſt-Indies*, and brought with him four Companies of Foot. In *September* of the ſame year Mr. *Courſel* arrived with the Commiſſion of Governor General of *Canada*, with eleven Veſſels, which tranſported a Regiment, and ſeveral Families, with all things neceſſary for the eſtabliſhing of a Colony. The *French* Force being thus ſo conſiderably augmented, he reſolved in the Winter to ſend out a Party againſt the *Mohawks*, which by the Cold, and their not knowing the uſe of Snow-Shoes, ſuffered very much, without doing any thing againſt the Enemy.

This Party fell in with *Schenectady*, a ſmall Town which *Corlaer* (a conſiderable Man among the *Dutch*)" had then newly ſettled. When they appear'd near *Schenectady* they were almoſt kill'd with Cold and Hunger, and the *Indians*, who then were in that Village, had

had entirely finished their Ruin, if *Corlaer*, (in Compassion of fellow *Christians*) had not contriv'd their escape. He had a mighty Influence over the *Indians*, and it is from him that all the Governors of *New-York* are call'd *Corlaer* by the Indians to this Day, tho' he himself never was Governor. He perswaded the Indians that this was but a small Party of the *French* Army, come to amuse them, that the great Body was gone directly towards their Castles, and that it was necessary for them immediately to go in Defence of their Wives and Children: which they did. As soon as the Indians were gone, he sent to the *French*, and supply'd them with Provisions to carry them back. The *French* Governor, in order to Reward so signal a Service, invited *Corlaer* to *Canada*, and, no doubt, with design to make use of his Interest with the Indians in some Project, in favour of the *French* Colony; but as he went through the Lake (by the French call'd *Champlain*) his Canoe was Overset, and he drowned. From this Accident that Lake has ever since been call'd *Corlaers Lake* by the People of *New-York*.

There is a Rock in this Lake, on which the Waves dash and fly up to a very great height, when the Wind blows strong; the *Indians* fancy, that an Old *Indian* lives under this Rock, who has the Power of the Winds, and

and therefore as they pafs this Rock in their Voyages through this Lake, they always throw a *Pipe* or fome *Tobacco*, or fomething elfe to this Old *Indian*, and pray a favourable Wind. The *Englifh* that often pafs with them, fometimes laugh at them; but they are fure to be told of *Corlaers Death* with a grave air. *Your great Country-man* Corlaer (fay they) *as he paffed by this Rock, jefted at our Fathers making Prefents to this Old* Indian, *and in derifion turn'd up his Back-fide towards the Rock, but this Affront coft him his Life.*

But the next Spring the Vice-Roy and the Governor, with 28 Companies of Foot, and all the Inhabitants of the Colony, marched into the Country of the *Mohawks*, with a defign to deftroy this Nation, which by the War not only prevented their Commerce with other Indians, but even prevented the Settlement of the Colony. This certainly was a bold Attempt, to march thus above 250 Leagues from *Quebeck*, through unknown Forrefts; but all they were able to do, was to burn fome of their Villages, and to Murder fome Old Men, that (like the Old *Roman* Senators) would rather dye than defert their Houfes.

This Expedition. however, gave the *Five Nations* Apprehenfions they had not before; for they never before that faw fo great a Number of *Europeans*, whofe Fire-Arms were extreamly

treamly Terrible, and they therefore thought proper to send and beg a Peace, which was concluded in 1667.

But they being naturally very Enterprizing and Haughty, a Party of the *Five Nations* met with a Party of the *French* a hunting, and quarrelled with them. The *French* Author does not inform us of the particulars: But it seems the *Indians* had the Advantage, for they kill'd several of the *French* and carried one Prisoner into their own Country. Monf. *De Courfel* sent to Threaten the *Five Nations* with War, if they did not deliver up these Murderers.

The *Five Nations* being at this time apprehensive of the *French* Power, sent *Agariata*, the Captain of the Company that did the Mischief, with forty others, to beg Peace; but Mr. *Courfel* was resolved to make an Example of *Agariata*. He therefore ordered him to be Hang'd, in the Presence of his Country-men," which kind of Death they having never seen before, it struck them with Terror, & the *French*, think that this Severity was a great means of preserving the Peace till the year 1683.

The *Dutch* having settled *New-York* in 1609. (which they call'd the *New-Netherlands*) they enter'd into an Alliance with the *Five Nations*, which continued without any Breach on either side," and were frequently useful to the

French,

French, in saving the *French* that were Prisoners from the Cruelty of the *Indians*, as before observed.

In 1664. *New-York* was taken by the *English*, who immediately entred into an Alliance and Friendship with the *Five Nations*, which has continued without the least Breach to this Day. History, I am afraid, cannot inform us of an Instance of the *Most Christian* or *Most Catholick King* Observing a League so strictly, and for so long a time as these *Barbarians* have done.

Both the *English* and *French* (Peace being every where settled) endeavour to extend their Commerce and Alliances among the *Indians* which lie to the Westward of *New-York*. The *French* in their Measures discover'd a Design of Conquering and Commanding; for Mr. *de Frontenac*, who had succeeded in the Government of *Canada* in the Year 1672, perswaded the *Indians* to allow him to build a Fort at *Cadarackui*, under the Notion of a Store for Merchandize and security for his Traders, and under the same pretence built small Forts at some other considerable Passes far in the Country.

The *English* and *Dutch* Prosecuted their Measures only with the Arts of Peace, by sending People among the *Indians* to gain their Affections, and to perswade them to come to *Albany* to Trade; but ev'n these honest Designs

Designs met with Obstruction, and had not so considerable Success, by reason of the War with the *Dutch*, as otherwise they might have had; for in the Year 1674. *New-York* being Surpriz'd by the *Dutch*, and Restor'd, the alterations in Government and of Masters, obstructed very much the designs of gaining the *Indians*. Their Trade was likewise considerably hindred by the War, which the *Five Nations* had with the (*c*) *River Indians*, which forced many of the *River Indians* to seek shelter among the *Utawawas*, who fell under the *French* Government.

At last the *English*, *Dutch* and *French* having made Peace in *Europe*, and the Governor of *New-York* likewise having obtain'd a Peace between the *Five Nations* and *Mahikanders* or *River Indians*, the *English* and *French* were at full liberty to prosecute their designs of extending their Commerce among the *Indians*, which both did with very considerable success and advantage to the Inhabitants of their Colonies.

But this Justice must be done to the *French*, that they far exceeded the *English* in the daring attempts of some of their Inhabitants, in travelling very far among unknown *Indians*,

---

(*c*) The *Indians* living on the Banks of *Hudsons River* within or near the *English* Settlements.

dians, difcovering new Countries, and every where fpreading the Fame of the *French* Name and Grandeur, by making themfelves the Arbitrators in all difference between the *Indian Nations*. The Sieur *Perot* deferves to be remember'd, who pufhed his Difcoveries as far as the *Putewatemies* and Indians living round the farther Lakes, with the greateft Fatigues and Danger. He acquired the Languages of many Nations, and brought them to *Canada* to Trade, before the Peace was made with the *Five Nations*. In the Year 1667 he accomparied the Officer that was fent to the Fall of *St. Mary*, to take Poffeffion of all that Country, in the name of the *French King*, in the prefence of many of the Sachems of the Nations that liv'd round the Lakes, where there was an Alliance agree'd to with the *French*," but (ev'n by the *French* Books) no Subjection was Promifed.

In the Year 1697." Mr. *De la Sale* built a Sloop or Bark of fixty Tons on *Ohfwego Lake*," and provided her with great Guns. He carried this Veffel as far as *Miffilimackinack*, and there loaded her with Furrs and Skins, and then went on the Difcovery of the *Mififfipi*. He only left five or fix *French* on board to carry her back to *Oniagara*: But the *Indians* entertain'd fuch a Jealoufy of this floating Caftle, that they refolv'd fecretly to deftroy it, it, tho' they expreſt nothing to Mr. *De la Sale*, but Admiration of the extraordinary Machine, and ſent for all the Nations round to come to ſeee it. When they were together they conſulted how to ſurprize and deſtroy it; and this deſign they kept ſo ſecret, not only before the Execution, that Mr. *De la Sale* had no ſuſpicion of it, but afterwards likewiſe, for it was long before it was known what bceame of this Veſſel. At firſt they thought of killing all the *French* among them, and throwing themſelves on the *Engliſh* for their Protection; but their Courage fail'd them. They thought they might act with more ſecurity after Mr. *De la Sale* and his Company ſhould be gone on their intended Diſcoveries. The *French* having no ſuſpicion of their deſigns, permitted a Number of *Indians* to come on board in a Bay where the Bark came to an Anchor, in her return, and the *Indians* taking advantage of their Numbers, and the ſecurity of the *French*, murder'd the Men and burnt the Veſſel."

The Courage and Reſolution of theſe Gentlemen ought to be taken Notice of, for their Honour, notwithſtanding that the *Engliſh* ſay, that the Barrenneſs and Poverty of *Canada* puſhes the Men of Spirit there upon

upon Enterprizes they would not attempt if they liv'd in the Province of *New-York*.

CHAP. III.

The Affairs of the Five Nations *with the Neighbouring* English *Colonies.*

THe *Five Nations* being now amply supply'd with Fire-Arms and Ammunition, give full swing to their War-like Genius, and therefore resolv'd to Revenge the Affronts they had at any time receiv'd from their Neighbours. The nearest Nations as they were attackt, commonly flying to those that were further off, the *Five Nations* pursued This, together with a desire they had of Conquering and of making all the Nations round them their Tributaries, or to acknowledge the *Five Nations* to be their Masters, made the *Five Nation* over-run the greatest part of *North-America*. They carried their Arms as far *South* as *Carolina*, and to the *Northward* of *New-England*, and as far West as the *River Misisipi*, over a vast Country which extends 1200 Miles in Length, from North to South, and about six hundred Miles in Breadth, and entirely Destroyed many Nations that made Resistance.

These

Thefe War-like Expeditions often prov'd Troublefom to the Colonies of *Virginia* and *Maryland*; for not only the Indians who were Friends to thofe Colonies, became Victims to the Fury of the *Five Nations*, but the *Chriftian* Inhabitants likewife were involv'd often in the fame Calamity.

For this reafon about the year 1677. the Government of *Maryland* fent Coll. *Courfey* to *Albany* to make a League of Friendfhip between *Virginia* and *Maryland* on the one part, and the *Five Nations* on the other;[10] but this League was soon fhaken by fome Parties of the *Oneydoes*, *Onondagas* and *Sennekas*, who were out when this Covenant was made, and were ignorant of it. One of thefe Parties met with the *Sufquehana Indians*,[11] who were in Friendfhip with *Maryland*, and fell upon them, kill'd four, and took fix Prifoners. Five of thefe Prifoners fell to the fhare of the *Sennekas*, who, as foon as they arriv'd in their Country, fent them back with Prefents, to fhew that they kept to their League with *Maryland*; but the *Oneydoes* detain'd the Prifoner they had.

Another Party that went againft the *Canageffe Indians* (Friends of *Virginia*) were furprized by a Troop of *Virginia* Horfe, who kill'd one Man and took a Woman Prifoner. The Indians in Revenge kill'd four of the Inhabi-

Inhabitants, and carried away their Scalps, with fix *Chriſtian* Priſoners."

The *Mohawks* all this while kept themſelves ſtrictly to their League, and ſuffered none of their Indians to go towards *Virginia* and *Maryland*.

There is reaſon to think that the *Dutch*, who lived at *Schenectady* at that time, ſpirited up the *Indians* againſt the *Engliſh*; For the Commander at *Albany* hearing that the *Five Nations*, (the *Oneydoes* eſpecially) were in an Alarm from ſome Jealouſy that they had entertain'd of the *Engliſh* at *New-York* ſent *Arnout* and *Daniel*, two Interpreters of the Indian Language, to per-ſwade them to come to *Albany*, in order to be aſſured of the *Engliſh* Friendſhip, and to have their Jealouſy remov'd. Which the Interpreters having happily brought to paſs, *Sweriſſe*, one of the chief Men or Sachims of the *Oneydoes* ex-cus'd his Country-men at *Albany*, the 15th of *February* 1678,9. as follows,

"*Father Corlaer*;

"WE are now come to ſpeak to you of
" ſome ſtrange Occurences that have
" lately happened.

" Laſt Harveſt one of our Indians, call'd,
" *Treuhtanendo*, went to *Schenectady* to buy
" goods; he was told of the Miſchief we had
" done

"done in *Virginia*; To which the People of
"*Schenectady* added, That the *English* of this
"Government were very Angry, and that
"they would kill us.

"Soon afterwards another of our Indians,
"call'd, *Adagounwa*, went to *Schenectady*, in
"his way to *Albany*; He was told by the
"People there, That if he went forward to
"*Albany* he might fing to Morrow, for the
"*English* there would bind and kill him;
"Whereupon he and another *Indian* immedi-
"ately returned, and brought this Report to
"to our Caftle at *Oneido*.

"But we now fee the Governors good heart,
"notwithftanding of all this bad News.

"At laft the People of *Schenectady* told five
"of our Indians, who intended for *Albany*,
"That if they went forward they would all
"be Dead Men; upon which one run im-
"mediately back, but the other four went
"forward. This Man, (who is called *Oun-
"wahraribta*) told us, That the other four
"Men were taken by the *English*, and that two
"or three hundred Men were upon their way
"to fight us. Upon hearing of this, I ac-
"knowledge, that though I, *Sweriffe*, be a
"Sachem, I left the Affair wholly to our
"Soldiers, feeing that they were Soldiers
"who came againft us; Whereupon our Men
"immediately Refolv'd to Fortifie the Caftle.

"While this was doing the War-Shout was "raised. Our Men call'd out, *That Horse-men "came against us; Now we shall be put to it.* "These prov'd to be the two Interpreters, "who being receiv'd into the Castle, our "young Soldiers, whose Spirits had been ve- "hemently raised, run round them with their "Hatchets in their hands, threatning to kill "them. But I, *Sweriffe*, did what I could to "pacifie our Men, and told the Messengers, "*That we would hear them to Morrow.*

"*Father Corlaer*; We desire that your Anger "may be appeased, and that your Mind may "be quieted. We give no credit to the "stories which our *Indians* brought us from "*Schenectady*, and we shall not believe any "such Stories for the future Seeing all of us "to the Westward, ev'n from *New-York* to the "*Sennekas*, are under one Government, Why "is *Schenectady* the only bad place? for We "hold firmly to the Old Covenant.

Then he gave a Belt of Wampum (*d*)

He

(*d*) *Wampum* is the current Money among the *Indians*, it is made of the large Whelk Shell (*Briccinum*) and shaped like long Beads. With this, put upon strings, they make these Belts, which they give in all their Treaties, as signs of Confirmation, to remain with the other Party. The Wampum is of two sorts, *viz. White* and *Black*; the *Black* is the rarest, and most valuable. By a regular mixing of the

Part I. *Indian Nations.*

He in the next place gave an account of what had happened in *Virginia,* And then said,

"*Father Corlaer*;

"Have Pity on our Indian Prisoners, as "We have had on these Prisoners (viz. *A Woman and her two Children*) "which we "now deliver to you, notwithstanding that "they have been giv'n away, according to "our Custom. We pray therefore his Ho-"nour to take Pity on our People that are "Prisoners, especially on the *Indian* Woman, "his Kins-Woman, whom he hath adopted as "a Grand-Child. Let them be Released, if "alive, otherwise give us some of the *Cana-*"*stoga Indians* in their room. As to the other "three Christian Prisoners, the Woman and "her two Children that are yet with us, We "desire first to have our Indians Restored, "or others in their room, before they be De-"livered.

---

the Black and White they distinguish their Belts with various Figures, which they often suit to the Occasion of making use of them. *Wompum* is called *Zewant* by the *Dutch* in this Province.

Governor *Andross*, being acquainted by Letter with this laſt Propoſal of the *Oneydoes*, required the immediate Delivery of the Chriſtian Priſoners, and promiſed to write to *Virginia* to have the *Indian* Priſoners ſaved. Some preſents being given to to the *Oneydoes*, they anſwered,

"We Thank the Governor for his good "Inclination and Affection. Our Heart is "good, and we ſee his Heart is likewiſe good; "if it was otherwiſe we could not live: We "thank theGovernor for the Preſent now giv'n "us: It is his wellcome from *England*.

"*Father Corlaer*, We are your Children, "and the *Mohawks*, your Brethren, are like- "wiſe our Fathers. We rejoyce becauſe your "Heartsare good. Since the Governor is "not ſatisfied with theſe three Priſoners, we "have now unanimouſly Reſolved to bring "the other three which are ſtill with us, as "ſoon as poſſible; but the Rivers are now ſo "full of Water, that we cannot bring them this "Moon, but the next Moon, I, *Sweriſſe*, pro- "miſe to come with them.

"We obey the Governor's Orders, that "we may not be aſhamed, and therefore We "Releaſe all the Priſoners. We hope the "Governor will likewiſe act ſo as he need "not be aſhamed.

"We do not now ſay, that we will ſee our
Priſoners

"Prisoners before we deliver the other Chri-
"stians, but refer this Affair wholly to the
"Governor's Wisdom, which, we hope, will
"tend to our good and continued Wellfair.
"And say again, That we will bring the three
"Christian Prisoners by the first opportunity
"of fair Weather.

"We likewise make known to our Father
"*Corlaer*, That in our Fury and Anger (after
"the People of the South had fallen upon us)
"We took these six Prisoners, and afterwards
"four Scalps were brought by our People,
"and no more.

"We speak as *Oneydoes*, for our selves. If
"the *Susquehana* or *Delaware* Indians have
"done any Mischief, let not that be impu-
"ted to us.

"Eight of our People are now out against
"the *Christians*, of which we told *Aernout*
"and *Daniel* when they were at our Castle.
"They know nothing of what we have
"now agree'd to, and therefore if they should
"happen to do any harm, let it be passed
"by, for they are entirely Ignorant of the
"Governor's Orders. If they shall do any
"thing, we shall not keep it secret. If any
"of the *Christian* Prisoners shall dye before
"we bring them, we should be sorry; yet
"they are Mortal."

Accordingly in *May* following the *Oneydoes*
brought

brought the other three Prisoners to *Albany*. And on the 24th of that Month *Sweriſſe* made the following Speech, when he deliver'd them to the Commander at *Albany*, and the Commiſſioners for *Indian* Affairs.

" *Bretheren*;

"WE are come to this place with much
" Trouble, as we did laſt Winter,
" and renew the Requeſt we then made, that
" ſix *Indians* be delivered to us in the room of
" the ſix *Chriſtians*, in caſe thoſe of our People
" who are Priſoners in *Virginia* be dead. None
" of our *Indians* have gone out againſt the
" *Engliſh* ſince we were laſt here; but we have
" told you that ſome of ours were then out, who
" were ignorant of the Governor's Orders,
" and we deſired that if they happen'd to
" do any harm, it might not be ill taken. Now
" thirteen of our People who went againſt
" our *Indian* Enemies, met with eighteen
" *Engliſh* on Horſeback, as far from any of
" the *Engliſh* Plantations as *Cahnuaga* (*e*) is
" from *Albany*. They fir'd upon our Peo-
" ple; ours being Soldiers, return'd their
" Fire and kill'd two Men and two Horſes,
" and brought away their Scalps.

" It would be convenient that the Gover-
" nor

(*e*) The firſt *Mohawk* Caſtle.

"nor acquaint the People of *Virginia*, not to
"send their Men so far abroad, for if they
"should happen to meet our Parties in their
"way against our Enemies, the *Cahnowas*,"
"whom the *English* call *Arogisti*, dangerous
"Consequences might follow.

"We have now submitted to the Gover-
"nor's Order, in bringing the three other
"Christian Prisoners. When we were here
"last Winter, we left the Affair of our Pri-
"soners wholy to the Governor, and pro-
"mised to bring the three Christian Priso-
"ners that remain'd with us. This we have
"now perform'd: But where are our Priso-
"ners, or if they be dead, the others in
"their room, tho' it be already so late in
"the Spring: However, we still refer this
"to the Governor.

(Then taking the *Christian* Girl, who was
a Prisoner, by the hand, said) "This Girl
"was deliver'd to an *Indian Squa* (*e*) here
"present, who's Brother then was kill'd.
"If we had been full of Wrath, and not
"afraid of further Inconveniencies, we would
"have burnt her.

(Taking the Boy, another of the three, by
the hand, said) "This Boy was giv'n to an
"*Indian* here present, but he is now free.
"We

(*f*) A Woman.

"We have now perform'd our Promises,
"and are not ashamed. We hope *Corlaer*,
"who Governs the whole Country, will
"likewise do that of which he needeth not
"be ashamed.

"*Corlaer* governs the whole Land, from
"*New-York* to *Albany*, and from thence to
"the *Sennekas* Land; We who are his Sub-
"jects shall faithfully keep the Covenant
"Chain: Let him perform his Promise, as
"we have perform'd ours, that the Covenant
"Chain be not broken on his side, who go-
"verns the whole Country.

"*Corlaers* Limits, as we have said, stretch
"so far ev'n to *Jacob my Friend*, or *Jacob
"Young*, and we have heard that *Corl er* is
"in good Correspondence with *Virginia* and
"*Maryland*; Why is it then that our Peo-
"ple, who are Prisoners, are not restored?
"Let what we now say be well observed,
"for we have observed the Governor's Or-
"ders.

Lastly (taking the Woman Prisoner by
the hand, said) "This Woman was given
"to that *Indian*, (*pointing*,) but is now free,
"being the sixth. If those of our People
"who are Prisoners be Dead, let us have six
"*Indians* in their room. It is not by my Au-
"thority that these Prisoners have been re-
"leased, but by the good Will of them to
"whom

"whom they were given.

"Our Soldiers are to go out againſt the "*Dewagunhas*, let us have Ammunition cheap."

Then the Commiſſioners gave them Preſents for their kind Uſage of the Priſoners.

After which *Swerſſe* ſtood up and ſaid, "Let *Corlaer* take care that the *Indian Squa* "that is wanting come again, and for thoſe "that are killed, others in their room. If "*Corlaer* will not hearken to us in this Affair, "we ſhall not hereafter hearken to him in "any."

They hearing afterwards that theſe laſt words were ill taken, *Swerſſe*, *Jehonongera* and *Kanohguage*, three of the chief *Oneydo* Sachems excuſed it, ſaying, "What we ſaid of not "hearkening any more to *Corlaer*, was not "from the heart, but only by way of Diſ-"courſe, to make *Corlaer* more careful to "releaſe our People that are Priſoners; for "it was ſaid after your Anſwer, and without "laying down either Bever or any Belt or "Wampum, as we always do when we make "(g) Propoſitions; Therefore we deſire that

---

(g) The word *Propoſition* has been always uſed by the Commiſſioners for *Indian* Affairs at *Albany*, to ſignifie *Propoſals* or *Articles*, in the Treaties or Agreements made with the *Indians*.

"if it be noted, it may be blotted out, and "not made known to *Corlaer*; for we hold "firmly to our Covenant, as we said in our "Propositions.

They at the same time told, That the *Sinnondowans* (*h*) came to them with eight Belts, desiring that they should no longer prosecute the War with *Virginia*, or *Virginia Indians*, but to go with them to War against the *Dowaganhas*, (*i*) a Nation lying to the North-westward; and that the *Sennekas* did desire them to set these *Christians* at Liberty, and to carry them to *Albany*. All which they said they promised to do.

The *Five Nations* continuing still to be troublesome to *Virginia*, that Government, in *September* following, sent Col. *William Kendall* and Col. *Southley Littleton* to *Albany*, to Renew and Confirm the League between *Virginia* and the *Five Nations*. Col. *Littleton* dy'd at *Albany* before the *Indians* arriv'd. Col. *Kendall* spoke to the *Oneydoes*, as follows,

---

(*h*) A Castle of the *Sennekas*, from whence the *French* call all the *Sennekas*, *Tsonontouan*.

(*i*) Comprehended under the General name of *Utawawas*.

The Propositions of Col. William Kendall *and Col.* Southley Littleton *Commissioners sent by the Governor, Council and Burgesses of* Virginia, *at a Grand Assembly held in* James-City.

"WE are come from *Virginia*, being, as all these Countries are, under the Great King *Charles*, to speak to you upon Occasion of some of yours having entred our Houses, taken away and destroy'd our Goods and People, and brought some of our Women and Children Captives into your Castles, contrary to your Faith and Promise. It is also a Breach of the Peace made with Col. *Coursey*, without any Provocation or Injury in the least done by us, or disturbing you in your Hunting, Trade, or Passing, until you were found taking our Corn out of our Fields, and plundering and burning our Houses.

"Tho' your Actions already done are sufficient Reasons to enduce us to a violent War against you, which might engage all our Confederate *English* Neighbours, Subjects to our great King *Charles*; yet through the great Respect we have to and the Perswasions of the Governor here, whom we find your great Friend, and the Information

"tion that he has given us, that you have
"quietly and peaceably deliver'd to him
"the Prisoners you had taken from us, who
"are also returned safely into our Country,
"and your Excusing the same, and Inclina-
"tion to continue Peaceable, without Inju-
"ring us for the future, We are therefore
"willing, and have, and do forgive all the
"Damages which you have done our Peo-
"ple, tho' very great, Provided neither you
"nor any living among you, for the future,
"do not offend or molest our People or In-
"dians living amongst us.

"And we do acquaint you, that we have
"a Law in our Country, that all *Indians*
"coming near *Christians* must stand still, and
"lay down their Arms, as a token of their
"being Friends, or otherwise are taken and
"lookt upon or destroyed as Enemies.
"Therefore desire you will take notice
"thereof accordingly, for we have many of
"our People in the Woods abroad every
"way.

He spoke to the *Mohawks*, and the other Nations seperately from the *Oneydoes*, because the other Nations were supposed not to have done any Mischief.

"We are come here from *Virginia* upon
"occasion of some of your Neighbours do-
"ing of Mischief or Harm in our Country,
"which

"which upon the Interpofition and Perfwa-
"fion of the Governour here, we have who-
"ly paffed by and forgiven. And being
"inform'd, that you are not concern'd there-
"in, but difowning fuch Actions, we did
"defire to fee you, and to let you know
"that continuing the like good peaceable
"Neighbourhood, you fhall find us the fame,
"and willing to do you Friendfhip at all
"times, but we muft acquaint you, that we
"have a Law, &c." (repeating the fame
words which he fpoke to the *Oneydoes* on
that fubject.)

On the Twentyfifth, he thought it neceffary to repeat this laft Speech to the *Mohawks*
by themfelves, who after they had receiv'd
fome Prefents, anfwered on the Twentyfixth
before Noon,

"WE are glad to fee you here, and to
" fpeak with you in this place, where
"we never faw you before. We underftood
"your Propofitions; We thank you for your
"Prefents and fhall give you an Anfwer After-
"noon.

In the Afternoon they faid,
" *Bretheren*;
"You have had no fmall trouble to come
"hither from *Virginia*, for it is a long Journey.
"We are at your requeft, and with our Go-
"vernors

"vernors Confent, come to meet you in this
"Houfe, which is appointed for our Treaties,
"to hear you fpeak, and to give you an An-
"fwer. But before we give an Anfwer, we
"make the appointed Houfe clean by giving
"this (*k*) Fathom of Wampum.

"We juft now faid, that your long Journey
"muft have not been without much Fatigue,
"efpecially to you who are an Old Man. I am
"old likewife, and therefore I give you this
"Fathom of Wampum to mitigate your pain.

"In the Beginning of your Speech you tell
"us of the League or Covenant made with
"Coll. *Courfey*. We remember it very well,
"that it was made in our Governors Prefence.
"We have kept it hitherto, and are refolv'd
"to keep it Inviolably. We are glad to fee
"you here, to renew this Covenant. You do
"better than the People of the *Eaft*, (*New-
"England*) who made a Covenant at the fame
"time; for we have feen none of them fince,
"to renew and keep up the Remembrance of
"it.' Then they gave a Fathom of Wampum.

"We have faid what we have to fay, as to
"the Covenant made with Coll. *Courfey*. You
"defire

(*k*) A Fathom of *Wampum* is a fingle ftring of *Wampum* of that length, it is of lefs value than the Belts, and therefore given in Matters of fmaller Confequence; and by cleaning the Houfe, they mean putting away *Hypocrefy* and *Deceit*.

"desire us likewise to continue our good
"Neighbourhood. This we not only pro-
"mise to do, but likewise to keep the (*l*)
"Chain, which cannot be broken, clean and
"bright, and therefore we desire you to do
"the same.' Then gave a Belt of Wampum
twelve deep.

"We are glad that by the Interposition
"and Perswasion of our Governor, the
"Mischeif which our Neighbours did in your
"Country is passed over, and now wholly
"forgiven. Let it be buried in Oblivion;
"for if any mischief should befal them
"(seeing we make but one body with them,)
"we must have partaken with them. We
"approve of your Law, to lay down our
"Arms as a token of Friendship, and we
"shall do so for the future.' Then gave a
Belt fourteen deep.

"We were told before we heard your
"Propositions, that one of the Agents from
"*Virginia* was Dead. We lament and bewail
"his Death, but admire that nothing was
"laid down, according to our Custom, when
"the Death of such a Person was signified to
"us. We give you this Belt of Black
"Wampum (thirteen deep) to wipe away
"your Tears. The

(*l*) The *Indians* always express a League by a Chain by which two or more things are kept fast together.

The *Onnondagas* did not come till *November*, on the 5th of which Month the *Virginia* Agent spoke to them in the same words he had done to the *Oneydoes*. None of their Answers appear upon the Registers, except the *Mohawks*, which we have given. It is certain that the *Onnondagas* and *Oneydoes* did not observe the Peace with *Virginia*, but molested them with the reiterated Incursions of their Parties. It is observable however, that these two Nations and the *Cayugas* only, had received *French Priests* among them, and that none of the rest who were not under the Influence of those Priests, ever molested the *English*; for which reason Coll. *Dongan*, tho' a *Papist*, complained of the ill Offices the Priests did to the *English* Interest, and forbid the *Five Nations* to entertain any of them, tho' the *English* and *French* Crowns, while he was Governor of *New-York*, in King *James*'s Reign, seem'd to be more than ever in strict Friendship."

The *French* could have no hopes of perswading the *Indians* to hurt any of the Inhabitants of *New-York*, but they were in hopes, that by the *Indian* Parties doing frequently Mischief in *Virginia*, the Government of *New-York* would be forced to joyn in resenting the Injury, and thereby that Union between the Government of *New-York* and the *Five Nations* would be broke, which always obstructed

ſtructed and often defeated the Deſigns of the *French*, to ſubject all *North-America* to the Crown of *France*. For this reaſon the Governors of *New-York* have always, with the greateſt Caution, avoided a Breach with theſe Nations, on account of the little Differences they had with the Neighbouring Colonys."

Theſe new Incurſions of these two Nations were ſo troubleſome to the People of *Virginia*, that their Governor, the Lord *Howard* of *Effingham*, thought it neceſſary for their Security, to undertake a Voyage to *New-York*.

The Sachems of the *Five Nations* being call'd to *Albany*, his Lordſhip met there eight *Mohawk*, three *Oneydoe*, three *Onnondaga* and three *Cayuga* Sachems, and on the Thirtieth of *July*, 1684. being accompanied with two of the Council of *Virginia*, he ſpoke to them as follows, in the preſence of Col. *Thomas Dongan*, Governor of *New-York*, two of the Council of *New-York*, and the Magiſtrates of *Albany*. The *Sennekas* living far off were not then arriv'd.

Propoſitions

Propositions made by the Right Honourable Francis
Lord Howard *of* Effingham, *Governor General of His Majesty's Dominion of* Virginia,
  To the Mohawks, Oneydoes, Onnondagas *and* Cayugas.

"IT is now about seven years ago since
"you (unprovok'd) came into *Virginia*, a
"Country belonging to the Great King of
"*England*, and committed several Murders
"and Robberys, carrying away our *Christian*
"Women and Children Prisoners into your
"Castles. All which Injurys we designed
"to have Revenged on you; but at the de-
"sire of Sir *Edmond Andross*, then Governor
"General of this Country, we desisted from
"destroying you, and sent our Agents Col.
"*William Kendall* and Col. *Southley Littleton*, to
"Confirm and make sure the Peace that Col.
"*Coursey* of *Maryland* included us in, when
"first he Treated with you. We find, that
"as you quickly forgot what you promised
"Col. *Coursey*, so you have willfully broke
"the Covenant Chain, which you promised
"our Agent, Col. *Kendall*, should be most
"strong and bright, if we of *Virginia*, would
"bury in the Pit of Oblivion, the Injurys
"you had then done us, which upon your
"Governor *Andross*'s Intercession, and your
                                      "Sub-

"Submiffion, we were willing to forget;
"But you not at all minding the Covenant
"then made, have every year fince, come into
"our Country, in a War-like manner, under
"pretence of Fighting with our *Indians*, our
"Friends and Neighbours, which you ought
"not to have done, our Agent having enclu-
"ded them likewife in the Peace. You not
"only deftroyed and took many of them
"Prifoners, but you have alfo kill'd and
"burnt our *Chriftian People*, deftroying our
"Corn and Tobacco, more than you made ufe
"of, killing our Horfes, Hogs and Cattle,
"not to eat, but let them ly in the Woods
"and ftink. This you did, when you were
"not denied anything you faid you want-
"ed.

"I muft alfo tell you that under the pre-
"tence of Friendfhip, you have come to our
"Houfes at the heads of our Rivers (where
"they have been fortified) with a white Sheet
"on a Pole, and have laid down your Guns
"before the Fort, upon which our People
"taking you to be Friends, have admitted
"your great Men into their Forts, and have
"given them Meat and Drink, what they
"defired. After the great Men had refrefhed
"themfelves, and defiring to return, as they
"were let out of the Fort Gates, the young
"Men rufhed into the Fort and plunder'd the

"Houfe,

" Houſe, taking away and deſtroying all the
" Corn, Tobacco, Bedding, and what elſe
" was in the Houſe. When they went away,
" they took ſeveral Sheep with them, and
" kill'd ſeveral Cows big with Calf, and left
" them behind them, cut to pieces and flung
" about, as if it were in Defiance of the Peace,
" and deſtroying of our Friendſhip.

" Theſe, and many more Injurys that you
" have done us, have cauſed me to raiſe
" Forces, to ſend to the heads of our Rivers
" to defend our People from your Outrages,
" till I came to *New-York* to Col. *Thomas Dongan*,
" your Governor General, to deſire him, as
" we are all one Kings Subjects, to aſſiſt me
" in Warring againſt you, to Revenge the
" *Chriſtian* Blood that you have ſhed, and to
" make you give full Satisfaction for all the
" goods that you deſtroyed. But by the
" Mediation of your Governor, I am now
" come to *Albany* to ſpeak with you, and to
" know the reaſon of your breaking the Cove-
" nant Chain, not only with us and our neigh-
" bour *Indians* but with *Maryland*, who are
" great King *Charles*'s Subjects; for our *Indians*
" have giv'n great King *Charles* their Land.
" Therefore I, the Governor of *Virginia*, will
" protect them, as your Governor under the
" Great *Duke* of *York* and *Albany*; will hence-
" forth you, when the Chain of Friendſhip is
" made between us all. " Now

Part I. *Indian Nations.* 53

"Now that I have let you know that I am "fenfible of all the Injurys that you have "done us, by the defire of your noble Go-"vernor General, I am willing to make a new "Chain with you for *Virginia, Maryland,* and "our *Indians,* that may be more ftrong and "lafting, even to the World's end, fo that "we may all be Bretheren and Great King "*Charles*'s Children.

"I propofe to you, *Firſt,* That you call "out of our Countrys of *Virginia* and *Mary-*"*land* all your young Men or Soldiers that "are now there.

"*Secondly,* That you do not hinder or moleſt "our Friend *Indians* from Hunting at our "Mountains, it having been their Country "and none of yours. They never go into "your Country to difturb any of you.

"*Thirdly,* Tho' the Damages you have "done our Country be very great, and "would require a great deal of Satisfaction, "which you are bound to give, yet we af-"fure you, that only by the Perfwafions of "your Governor, who is at a vaft deal of "Trouble and Charge for your Wellfare, "which you ever ought to acknowledge, "I have paffed it by and forgiven you, "upon this Condition, that your People, "nor any living among you, never commit "any Incurfions on our *Chriſtians* or *Indians*
"living

"living among us, or in *Maryland*.

"For the better Confirmation of the fame and that the Peace now concluded, may be lafting, I propofe to have two (*m*) Hatchets buried as a final Determination of all Wars and Jarrings between us: One on behalf of us and our *Indians*, and the other for all your Nations united together, that ever did us any Injury, or pretended to War againft our *Indian* Friends or *Maryland*.

"And that nothing may be wanting for Confirmation thereof, (if you defire it) we are willing to fend fome of our *Indian* Sachems with an Agent next Summer, about this time, that they may Ratifie the Covenant with you here in this prefixed Houfe, where you may fee and fpeak together as Friends.

"That the Covenant now made between us in this prefixed Houfe, in the prefence of your Governor, may be firmly kept and perform'd on your parts, as it always has on ours, and that you do not break any one Link of the Covenant Chain for the future, by your Peoples coming near our Plantations; When you march to the
"South-

(*m*) All Indians make ufe of the Hatchet or Ax as an emblem to exprefs War.

"Southward, keep to the feet of the Moun-
"tains, and not come nigh the heads, of our
"Rivers, there being no Bever Hunting
"there; for we fhall not for the future
"(tho' you lay down your Arms as Friends)
"ever truft you more, you have fo often
"deceiv'd us.

The next Day the Mohawks *anfwered firft by their Speaker, faying,*

"WE muft, in the firft place, fay
" fomething to the other three Na-
"tions by way of Reproof for their not keep-
"ing the former Covenant, as they ought,
"and therefore we defire you, great Sachem
"of *Virginia*, and you *Corlaer*, and all Peo-
"ple here prefent, to hearken, for we will
"conceal nothing of the Evil they have done.
(Then turning to the other three Nations)
"You have heard Yefterday all that has been
"faid; as for our parts, we are free of the blame
"laid on us for the Mifchief done in *Virgi-
"nia* and *Maryland*. You are Stupid, Bru-
"tifh, and have no Underftanding, thus to
"break your Covenant. We have always
"been obedient to *Corlaer*, and have fteadily
"kept our Covenant with *Virginia*, *Mary-
"land* and *Bofton*; we muft therefore Stamp
"Underftanding into you. Let the Cove-
"nant

"nant made Yesterday, be carefuly kept for the future. This we earnestly recommend to you; for we are ready to cry, for shame of you. Let us be no more ashamed on your Account, but be obedient, and take this Belt to keep what we say in your Remembrance.

"Hear now, now is the time to hearken. The Covenant Chain had very near slipt. You have not obferv'd your Covenant. Observe it now, when all former Evil is buried in the Pit.

"You *Oneydoes*, I speak to you as (*n*) Children. Be no longer void of Understanding.

"You *Onnondagas*, our Bretheren, you are like Deaf People, that cannot hear, your Senses are cover'd with Dirt and Filth.

"You *Cayugas*, Do not return into your former ways. There are three things we must all observe.

"*First*, The Covenant with *Corlaer*. *Secondly*, The Covenant with *Virginia* and *Maryland*. *Thirdly*, The Covenant with *Boston*. We must Stamp Understanding into you, that you may be obedient. And Take this Belt for a Remembrancer.

Then

(*n*) The *Mohawks* always call the *Oneydoes* Children, and the *Oneydoes* acknowledge the *Mohawks* to be their Fathers.

Then *Odianne*, the same *Mohawk* Speaker, turning to my Lord, spoke in behalf of all the four Nations.

"We are very thankful to you, great Sachem "of *Virginia*, that you are pleased to be per- "swaded by *Corlaer*, our Governor, to forgive "all former Faults. We are very glad to hear "you and to see your Heart softned. Take "these three Bevers as a Token.

"We thank the great Sachem of *Virginia* "for saying, that the Ax shall be thrown into "the Pit. Take these two Bevers as a Token "of our Joy and Thankfulness.

"We are glad that (*o*) *Assarigoa*," will bury "in the Pit what is past, and stamp thereon. "Let a strong stream likewise run under the "Pit, to wash the evil all away. *Gives* 2 *Bevers*.

"My Lord, you are a Man of great Know- "ledge and Understanding, thus to keep the "Covenant Chain bright as Silver, and now "again to Renew it, and make it stronger.

(Then pointing to the othe three Nations said,) "But they are Covenant Breakers. I "lay down this as a Token that we *Mohawks* "have kept the Covenant entire on out parts. Giving two Bevers and a Raccoon.

"The Covenant must be kept; for the fire "of

(*o*) The Name, which the *Five Nations* always give the Governors of *Virginia*.

"of Love of *Virginia* and *Maryland* burns in
"this place, as well as ours, and this Covenant
"House must be kept clean. Gives two
Bevers.

"We now plant a (*p*) Tree, who's tops
"will reach the Sun, and its Branches spread
"far abroad, so that it shall be seen afar off; &
"we shall shelter ourselves under it, and live in
"Peace, without molestation. *Gives two Bevers.*

"You proposed yesterday, that if we were
"desirous to see the *Indians* of *Virginia*, you
"are willing to send some of their Sachems
"next Summer about this time to this Place.
"This Proposal pleases us very much. The
"sooner they come, it will be the better, that
"we may speak with them in this House, which
"is apointed for our speaking with our Friends.
And gave two Belts to confirm it.

"You have now heard what Exhortation we
"have made to the other three Nations. We
"have taken the Hatchet out of their hands.
"We now therefore pray, that your Hatchet
"may likewise be buried in the Pit. Giving
two Bevers,

"Let the River be secure, for we some-
"times make Propositions to the *Raritan* and
"*Nevessink Indians*; but above all, let your
"*Virginia Indians* come securely hither, that
"we

(*p*) The *Five Nations* always express *Peace* under the Metapher of a *Tree*, in this manner.

"we may keep a good Correspondence with
"them.

"*My Lord*, Some of us *Mohawks* are out
"against Our Enemies that live a far off.
"When they come near your Plantations,
"they will do you no harm, nor Plunder as
"the others do. Be kind to them, if they
"shall happen to come to any of your Plan-
"tations. Give them some Tobacco and some
"Victuals; for they will neither Rob nor
"Steal, as the *Oneydoes, Onnondagas* and *Cayugas*
"have done.

"The *Oneydoes* particularly Thank your
"Lordship for hearkening to lay down the
"Ax. The Hatchet is taken out of all their
hands. And gives a Belt.

"We again thank your Lordship, that the
"Covenant Chain is Renewed. Let it be kept
"clean and bright, and held fast, Let not any
"one pull his Arm from it. We enclude all
"the *Four Nations* in giving this Belt.

"We again pray your Lordship, to take
"the *Oneydoes* into your Friendship, and that
"you keep the Covenant Chain strong with
"them; for they are in our Covenant. Gives
a Belt.

The *Oneydoes* give twenty Bevers, as satisfaction for what they promised my Lord *Baltimore*, and desire that they may be Discharged.

My Lord and the Governor told them, That they would use their Endeavours with the Lord *Baltimore*, to perswade him to forgive what remained.

Then the *Indians* desired that the Hole might be digged, to bury the Axes, *viz.* One in behalf of *Virginia* and their *Indians*, another in behalf of *Maryland* and their *Indians*, and three for the *Oneydoes*, *Onnondagas* and *Cayugas*. The *Mohawks* said, there was no need of burying any on their Account; for the first Chain had never been broke by them.

Then the three Nations spoke by an *Onnondaga*, call'd *Thanohjanihta*, who said,

"We Thank the great Sachem of *Virginia*, "that he has so readily forgiven and forgot "the Evil that has been done; And We, on " our parts, gladly catch at, and lay hold of the ". Chain." Then each of them deliver an Ax to be buried, and gave a Belt.

The Speaker added, "I speak in the Name " of all three Nations, and inculde them in " this Chain, which we desire may be kept " clean and bright like Silver. Gives a Belt.

" We desire that the Path may be open for " the *Indians*, under your Lordships Protection " to come safely and freely to this place, in " order to confirm this Peace·" Gives six Fathom of Wampum.

Then the Axes were buried in the South-east

eaſt end of the Court-yard, and the *Indians* threw the Earth upon them. After which my Lord told them, *That ſince now a firm Peace was concluded, We ſhall hereafter remain Friends, and* Virginia *and* Maryland *will ſend once in two or three years to Renew it, and ſome of Our* Indian *Sachems ſhall come, according to your deſire, to Confirm it.*

Laſt of all, the *Oneydoes, Onnondagas* and *Cayugas,* joyntly, ſang the *Peace Song,* with Demonſtrations of much Joy; and Thank'd the Governor of *New-York* for his effectual Mediation with the Governor of *Virginia,* in their favour.

The *Mohawks* by themſelves, and the other three Nations by themſelves, ſpoke to the Governor of *New-York,* much to the ſame purpoſe that they did to the Governor of *Virginia,* ſo far as it related to the Affair of *Virginia,* but with ſome particular Marks of Perſonal Eſteem; for he had won their Affections by his former carriage towards them. And they deſired the *Duke of York*'s Arms to put upon their Caſtles. Which, we may ſuppoſe, they were told, would ſave them from the *French.*

Coll. *Dongan* deſired them to call home thoſe

of

of their Nations that had settled in Canada. (*q*) To which they answered, '*Corlaer* keeps a 'Correspondence with *Canada*, and therefore 'he can prevail more than we can. Let *Corlaer* 'use his endeavours to draw our *Indians* home 'to their own Country.' And gave a Bever.

At the same Time, the Government of the the *Massachusets-Bay* had appointed Coll. *Stephanus Cortlandt*, one of the Council of *New-York*, their Agent, to Renew their Covenant with the *Five Nations*, and to give them some small Presents: Which was accordingly done.

The Governor of *New-York*, Coll. *Dongan*, concluded all, with this Advice to them, *Keep a good Understanding among your Selves: If any Difference should happen, acquaint me with it, and I will compose it. Make no Covenant or Agreement with*

(*q*) The *French* Priests had (from time to time) perswaded several of the *Five Nations* to leave their own Country, and to settle near *Montreal*, where the *French* are very industious in encouraging them. Their Numbers have been likewise encreased by the Prisoners the *French* have taken in War, and by others who have run from their own Country, because of some Mischief that they had done, or Debts which they ow'd to the *Christians*. These *Indians* all profess *Christianity*, and therefore are commonly call'd *The Praying Indians* by their Country-men, and they are called *Cahnuagas* by the People of *Albany*.[47]

Part I.   *Indian Nations.*   63

with the French, *or any other Nation, without my Knowledge or Approbation.* Then he gave the Dukes Arms, to be put upon each of their Castles, in hopes it might deter the *French* from attacking them (as they were threaten'd from *Canada*) after they had so manifestly declared themselves to be under the Protection of the Crown of *England*.

Before I proceed further it will be necessary to incert a Remarkable Speech made by the *Onnondagas* and *Cayugas*, to the two Governors, on the 2d day of *August, viz.*

Brother Corlaer ;

"YOur Sachem is a great Sachem, and We
" are but a small People. But when the
" *English* came first to *Manhatan*, (*r*) *Aragiske*,
" (*s*) and to *Yakokranagary*, (*t*) they were
" then but a Small People, and we Great.
" Then, because we found you a good People,
" we treated you civilly, and gave you Land.
" We hope therefore, now that you are Great
" and we Small, you will protect us from the
" *French*. If you do not, we shall loose all
" our Hunting, and our Bevers. The *French*
                                                    " will

(*r*) *New-York.*   (*s*) *Virginia.*   (*t*) *Maryland.*

"will get all the Bever. They are now angry
"with us, because we carry our Bever to our
"*Brethren*.

"We have put our Lands and our Selves
"under the Protection of the great *Duke of*
"*York*, the Brother of your great Sachem, who
"is likewife a great Sachem.

"We have given the *Sufquehana River*,
"which We won with the Sword, to this
"Government, and we defire that it may be
"a Branch of the great Tree that grows in
"this Place, the top of which reaches the
"Sun, and its Branches fhelter us from the
"*French*, and all other Nations. Our Fire
"burns in your Houfes, and your Fire burns
"with us. We defire that it may always be
"fo.

"We will not that any of the great *Penn*'s
"People fettle upon the *Sufquehana River*; for
"we have no other Land to leave to our Chil-
"dren.

"Our young People are Soldiers, and when
"they are difobliged they are like Wolves in
"the Woods, as you Sachem of *Virginia* very
"well know.

"We have put our Selves under the great
"Sachem *Charles*, that lives on the other fide
"of the great Lake. We give you thefe two
"White dreft Deer-Skins to be fent to the
"great Sachem, that he may write on them,
"and

" and put a great Red Seal to them, to Confirm
" what We now do, and put the *Sufquehana*
" *River* above the *Wafuhta* (*u*) and all the reft
" of our Land under the great *Duke of York*,
" and give that Land to no body elfe. Our
" *Brethren*, his People, have been like Fathers
" to our Wives and Children, and have given
" us Bread, when we were in need of it:
" We will not therefore joyn our felves or
" our Lands to any other Government but
" this. We defire *Colaer*, our Governor,
" may fend over this Propofition to the great
" Sachem, *Charles*, who dwells on the other
" fide the great Lake, with this Belt of Wam-
" pum, and this other fmaller Belt to the *Duke*
" *of York*, his Brother; And we give you,
" *Corlaer*, this Beaver, to fend over this Pro-
" pofition.

" You great Man of *Virginia*, We let you
" know, that great *Penn* did fpeak to us here
" in *Corlaers* Houfe, by his Agents, and de-
" fired to buy the *Sufquehana River* of us, but
" we would not hearken to him; for we
" had faften'd it to this Government. We
" defire of you therefore, that you would
" bear Witnefs of what we now do, and that
" we now Confirm what we have done be-
" fore. Let your Friend, the great Sachem
" that

(*u*) The Falls.

"that lives on the other side the great Lake,
"know this, that We being a Free People,
"tho' united to the *English*, may give our
"Lands, and be joyn'd to the Sachem we like
"best. We give this Bever to Remember
"what we say.

The *Senekas* arrived soon after, and on the 5th of *August* spoke to my Lord *Howard* in the following manner.

"WE have heard and understood what
"   Mischief hath been done in *Vir-*
"*ginia*. We have it as perfect as if it were
"upon our Fingers ends. O *Corlaer!* We
"Thank you for having been our Intercessor,
"so that the Ax hath not fallen upon Us.

"And you, *Assarigoa*, great Sachem of *Vir-*
"*ginia*, We Thank you for burying all Evil
"in the Pit. We are inform'd, that the
"*Mohawks, Oneydoes, Onnondagas* and *Cayugaes*
"have buried the Ax already; Now we that
"live the remotest off, are come to do the
"same, and to include in this Chain the *Cah-*
"*nawaas*, your Friends, who live amongst
"you. We desire therefore, that an Ax, on our
"part, may be buried with one of my Lords.
"O *Corlaer! Corlaer!* We Thank you for
"holding one end of the Ax: And We thank
"you, great Governor of *Virginia*, not only
                                            "for

"for throwing aſide the Ax, but more eſpe-
"cially for your putting all Evil from your
"Heart. Now we have a New Chain, a
"ſtrong and a ſtreight Chain that cannot be
"broken. The *Tree of Peace* is planted ſo
"firmly that it cannot be moved. Let us on
"both ſides hold the Chain faſt.

"We underſtand what you ſaid of the
"great Sachem that lives on the other ſide
"the great Water.

"You tell us, that the *Cahnawaas* will
"come hither to ſtrengthen the Chain. Let
"them not make any Excuſe, that they are
"Old and Feeble, or that their Feet are Sore.
"If the Old Sachems cannot, let the Young
"Men come. We ſhall not fail to come
"hither, tho' we live the fartheſt off, and
"then the New Chain will be ſtronger and
"brighter.

"We underſtand, that becauſe of the Miſ-
"chief which has been done to the People
"and Cattle of *Virginia* and *Maryland*, we
"muſt not come near the Heads of your
"Rivers, nor near your Plantations, but keep
"at the foot of the Mountains; for tho' we
"lay down our Arms, as Friends, we ſhall
"not be truſted for the future, but look'd on
"as Robbers. We agree, however, to this
"Propoſition, and ſhall wholly ſtay away
"from *Virginia*: And this we do in gratitude
"to

"to *Corlaer*, who has been at so great Pains to perswade you, *Great Governor of Virginia*, to forget what is past. We commend your Understanding, in giving ear to *Corlaer*'s goodAdvice; and we shall go a path which was never trod before.

"We have now done speaking to *Corlaer*, and theGovernor of *Virginia*. Let theChain be forever kept clean and bright, and we shall do the same.

"The other Nations, from the *Mohawks* Country to the *Cayugas*, have deliver'd up the *Susquehana River*, and all that Country, to *Corlaer*'s Government. We Confirm what they have done, by giving this Belt. "Ten Bevers are at the *Onnondagas* Castle in their way hither; We design five of them for *Corlaer*, and the other five for the Sachem of *Virginia*.

Coll. *Bird*, one of the Council of *Virginia*, and *Edmond Jennings*, Esq; Attorney General of that Province, came with four *Indian* Sachems, (according to my Lord *Howard*'s Promise) to Renew and Confirm the Peace, and met the *Five Nations* at *Albany* in *September*, 1685.

Coll. *Bird* accus'd them of having again broke their Covenant, by taking an *Indian* Girl from

from an *English* Mans Houfe, and four *Indian* Boys Prifoners.

They excufed this, by its being done by the Parties that were out when the Peace was concluded, who knew nothing of it; Which Accidents they had provided againſt in their Articles. They faid, The four Boys were given to the Relations of thofe Men that were loſt, and it would be very difficult to obtain their Reſtoration. But they promifed to deliver them up.

The *Senekas* and *Mohawks* declared themfelves free of any blame, and chid the other Nations.

So that we may ſtill obferve the Influence which the *French Priests* had obtain'd over thofe other Nations, and to what Chriſtian-like Purpofes they us'd it.

The *Mohawks* Speaker faid, *Where ſhall I ſeek the Chain of Peace? Where ſhall I find it, but upon Our Path? And whither doth Our Path lead us, but unto this Houfe? This is a Houfe of Peace.* And fang all the Covenant Chain over. He afterwards fang by way of Admonition to the *Onnondagas, Cayugas* and *Oneydoes,* and concluded all with a Song to the *Virginia Indians.* But I fuppofe our Interpreters were not Poets enough to Tranſlate the Songs, otherwife I might have gratified the Reader with a taſte of *Indian Poetry.*

The *French Priests* still had an Influence over the *Onnondagas*, *Cayugas* and *Oneydoes*, and it was eafie for them to fpirit up the *Indians* (naturally Revengeful) againft their old Enemies. This occafion'd a Party of the *Oneydoes* going out two years afterwards againft the *Wayanoak Indians*, Friends of *Virginia*, and killing fome of the People of *Virginia*, who affifted thofe *Indians*. They took fix Prifoners, which they reftored at *Albany*, with an Excufe, That they did not know that they were Friends of *Virginia*, and included in the Chain with *Virginia*. Coll. *Dongan*, on this Occafion, told them, That he only had kept all the *Englifh* in *North-America* from joyning together to Deftroy them; And at the fame time threatned them, That if ever he fhould hear of the like Complaint, he would dig up the Hatchet, and joyn with the reft of the *Englifh* to cut them off, Root and Branch; for there were many Complaints made of him to the King by the *Englifh*, as well as the Governor of *Canada*, for his favouring of them.

Now we have gone through the Material Tranfactions which the *Five Nations* had with the *Englifh*, in which we find the *Englifh* purfuing nothing but *Peaceable* and *Chriftian Meafures*, and the *Five Nations* (tho' *Barbarians*) living like good Neighbours and faithful Friends,

Friends, except when they were influenced by the Arts of the Jesuits; Tho' at the same time one cannot but admire the Zeal, Courage and Resolution of these Jesuits, that would adventure to live among *Indians* at War with their Nation; and the better to carry their Purposes, to comply with all the Humors and Manners of such a Wild People, so as not to be distinguished by strangers from meer *Indians*. One of them, nam'd *Milet*, remain'd with the *Oneydoes* till after the year 1694. he was advanced to the degree of a Sachem, and had so great an Influence over them, that the other Nations could not prevail with them to part with him. While he remain'd with them, the *Oneydoes* were frequently turn'd against the *Southern Indians* (Friends of the *English* Southern Colonies) and were always wavering in their Resolutions against *Canada*."

We shall now Return to see what effect the *French Policy* had, who pursued very different Measures from the *English*.

CHAP

CHAP. IV.

Mr. De la Barre's *Expedition, and some Remarkable Transactions in* 1684.

THe *French* in the Time they were at Peace with the *Five Nations*, built their Fort at *Teiodondoraghi* or *Missilimakinak*, and made a Settlement there. They carried their Commerce among the Numerous Nations that live on the Banks of the great *Lakes*, and the Banks of the *Misissipi*. They not only prosecuted their Trade among these Nations, but did all they could to secure their Obedience, and to make them absolutely subject to the *Crown of France*, by building Forts at the considerable Passes, and placing small Garrisons in them. They took all the Precautions in their Power, not only to restrain the *Indians* by Force, but likewise to gain their Affections, by sending Missionaries among them. The only Obstruction they met with, was from the *Five Nations*, who introduced the *English* of *New-York* into the Lakes, to Trade with the *Indians* that liv'd round them. This gave the *French* much uneasiness, because they fore-saw, that the *English* would not only prove dangerous Rivals, but that the Advantages which

which they enjoy'd in Trade, beyond what it was poffible for the Inhabitants of *Canada* to have, would enable the People of *New-York* fo far to under-fell them, that their Trade would foon be Ruin'd, and all the Intereft loft which they had gain'd with fo much Labour and Expence. The *Five Nations* likewife continued in War with many of the Nations, the *Chictaghiks* particularly, who yielded the moft Profitable Trade to the *French*; and as often as they difcover'd any of the *French* carrying Ammunition towards thefe Nations, they fell upon them, and took all their Powder, Lead and Arms from them. This made the *French* Traders afraid of traveling, and prevented their *Indians* from hunting, and leffen'd the Opinion they had of the *French Power*, when they found that the *French* were not able to protect them againft the Infults of the *Five Nations*.

The *Sennekas* lie next to the Lakes, and neareft to the Nations with whom the *French* Traded, and were fo averfe to the *French* Nation, that they never would receive any Prieft[50] among them, and of confequence were moft firmly attached to the *Englifh Intereft*, who fupplyed them with Arms and Powder, (the means to be Revenged of their Enemies.) For thefe reafons Mr. *De la Barre* (the Governor of *Canada*) fent a Meffenger to Coll. *Dongan*

Dongan, to complain of the Injuries the *Sennekas* had done to the *French*, and to show the necessity he was under to bring the *Five Nations* to Reason by Force of Arms; which Messenger happening to arrive at the time the *Indians* met my Lord *Howard* at *Albany*, Coll. *Dongan* told the *Sennekas* of the Complaints that the *French* Governor made of them. They gave him the following Answer, in Presence of Mr. *De la Barre*'s Messenger, on the 5th of *August*, 1684.

"WE were sent for, and are come, and
" have heard what you have said to us, That
" *Corlaer* hath great Complaints of us, both
" from *Virginia* and *Canada*. What they com-
" plain of from *Canada*, may possibly be true,
" that our Young People have taken some of
" their Goods; but *Yonnondio* is the cause of
" it. He not only permits his People to
" carry Ammunition, Guns, Powder, Lead &
" Axes to the *Tuihtuihronoon* (*x*) our Enemys,
" but sends them thither on purpose. These
" Guns which he sends knock our Bever-
" hunters on the head, and our Enemies carry
" the

(*x*) *Ronoon* signifies Nation or People, in the Language of the *Five Nations*, they say *Twihtwih-ronoon, Chiftag-hik-ronoon, Dedonondadik-ronoon, &c.*

"the Bevers to *Canada*, that we would have
"brought to our Brethren. Our Bever-
"hunters are Soldiers, and could bear this no
"longer. They met with some *French* in
"their way to our enemies, and very near
"them, carrying Ammunition, which our
"Men took from them. This is agreeable
"to our Customs of War, and we may there-
"fore openly own it; tho' we know not
"whether it be practised by the *Christians* in
"such like cases.

"When the Governor of *Canada* speaks to
"us of the Chain, he calls us *Children*, and
"saith, *I am your Father, you must hold fast
"the Chain, and I will do the same. I will
"Protect you as a Father doth his Children.* Is
"this Protection, to speak thus with his
"Lips, and at the same time to knock us on
"the head, by assisting our Enemies with
"Ammunition?

"He always says, *I am your Father, and
"you are my Children*, and yet he is angry
"with his Children for taking these goods.
But, O *Corlaer!* O *Assarigoa!* We must com-
"plain to you. You, *Corlaer*, are a Lord,
"and Governs this Country; Is it just that
"our Father is going to fight with us for
"these things, or is it well done? We rejoyced
"when *La Sal* was sent over the great Water,
"and when *Perot* was removed, because they
"had

"had furnished our Enemies with Ammuni-
"tion; but we are difapointed in our hopes;
"for we find that our Enemies are ftill
"fupplied. Is this well done? Yea, he often
"forbids us to make War on any of the
"Nations with whom he Trades, and at the
"fame time furnifhes them with all forts of
"Ammunition, to enable them to deftroy
"us.

"Thus far in Anfwer to the Complaints
"which the Governor of *Canada* hath made of
"Us to *Corlaer*. *Corlaer* faid to us, that
"Satisfaction muft be made to the *French* for
"the Mifchief we have done them. This
"he faid before he heard our Anfwer. Now
"let him that hath Infpection over all
"our Countries, on whom our Eyes are
"fix'd, let him, ev'n *Corlaer* judge and de-
"termine. If you fay it muft be paid, we
"fhall pay it, but we cannot live without
"free Bever-hunting.

"*Corlaer*, Hear what we fay, We Thank
"you for the Dukes Arms which you have
"given us to be put on our Caftles, as a De-
"fence to them. You command them. Have
"we wander'd out of the way, as the Go-
"vernor of *Canada* fays. We do not threaten
"him with War, as he threatens us. What
"fhall we do? Shall we run away, or fhall
"we fit ftill in our Houfes? What fhall we
"do?

Part I.   *Indian Nations.*   77

"do? We speak to him that Governs and
"Commands us.

"Now *Corlaer* and *Affarigoa*, and all People
"here prefent, Remember what we have
"anfwered to the Complaints of the Gover-
"nor of *Canada*; Yea, let what we fay come
"to his Ears." Then they gave a Belt, and
faid, there was five Bevers at *Onondaga* for the
Governor.

Monf. *De la Barre* at this time was gone
with all the Force of *Canada* to *Cadaraekui
Fort*, and order'd the three Veffels to be repair-
ed, which the *French* had built on that Lake.
His defign was to frighten the *Five Nations* into
his own Terms by the Appearance of fo great
an Army, which confifted of 600 Soldiers,
400 Indians, and 400 Men that carried Provifions, befides 300 Men that he left to fecure
Cadarackui Fort.[52] But while he was at this
Fort, the Fatigue of Traveling in the Month
of *Auguft* together with the Unhealthinefs of
that place (the Country thereabout being
very Marfhy) where he tarryed six weeks,
occafioned fo great a Siknefs in his Army, that
he found himfelf unable to Perform any
thing, but by Treaty, and therefore fent
Orders to Monf. *Dulhut*, who was come from
Miffilimakinak with 600 men *French* and *Indians*,
to ftop. He paffed a Crofs the Lake with as
many men as were able to Travel, and arrived
at

at the River which the *French* call *La Famine*, and by the *Indians* call'd *Kaihohage*," which runs from the *Onnondaga* and *Oneydo* Countrys, and falls into *Cadarackui Lakes*. There were two Villages of the *Five Nations* on the North fide of the Lake, about five or fix Leagues from the *French* Fort, confifting of thofe *Indians* that had the moft Inclination to the *French*: They provided the *French* Army with Provifions, while they remain'd at the Fort; but it is probable, fent an account to their own Nations of every thing that happen'd, which was the Reafon of the Ufage they afterwards met with from the *French*.

When Mr. *De la Barre* fent to Coll. *Dongan*, he was in hopes, from the ftrict Alliance that was then between the Crowns of *England* and *France*, and from Coll. *Dongan*'s being a *Papift*, that he would fit ftill till he had reduced the *Five Nations*. But none of thefe Reafons permitted that Gentleman to be eafie while the *French* attempted fuch things, as in their confequence would be to the higheft degree Prejudicial to the *Englifh Intereft*, & put all the *Englifh* Colonies in *America* in danger. Wherefore he difpatch'd the Publick Interpreter," with Orders to do every thing in his Power to prevent the *Five Nations* going to Treat with Mr. *De la Barre*.

The Interpreter fucceeded in his Defign
with

with the *Mohawks,* and with the *Sennekas,* who promis'd that they would not go near the *French* Governor. But he had not the like Succefs with the *Onnondagas, Oneydoes* and *Cayugas,* who had receiv'd the *French Priefts.* For they would not hear the Interpreter, but in Prefence of the *French Prieft,* and of Mr. *Le Maine,* whom the Indians call *Ohqueffe*" (y) and three other *French Men,* that Mr. *De la Barre* had fent to perfwade them to meet him at *Kaihohage,* ten Leagues from the *Onnondaga* Caftle. They gave the following Anfwer to the Interpreter.

Arie, You are *Corlaer's* Meffenger? *Ohqueffe*
" is the Governor of *Canada's;* and there fits
" our Father" (z) *Yonnondio* acquainted us
" fome time ago, that he would fpeak with
" us before he would undertake any thing
" againft the *Sennakas.* Now he hath fent for
" all the Nations to fpeak with him in Friend-
" fhip, and that at a Place not far from *Onnon-*
" *daga,* ev'n at *Kaihohage.* But our Brother
" *Corlaer* tells us, That we muft not meet the
" Governor of *Canada* without his Permif-
" fion; and that if *Yonnondio* have any thing
" to fay to us, he muft firft fend to *Corlaer* for
" leave to fpeak with us. *Yonnondio* has fent
" long ago to us to fpeak withhim, and he has
" lately

(y) That is, the Partridge. (z) Pointing to the Jefuit.

"lately repeated that Defire, by *Onniſſantie*,"
"the Brother of our Father *Twirhaerſira*, that
"fits there. He has not only intreated us by
"our Father, but by two *Praying Indians*, one
"an *Onnondaga*, the other the Son of an Old
"*Mohawk* Sachem, *Connondowe*. They
"brought five great Belts of Wampum, not
"a Fathom or two only, as you bring. Now
"*Ohqueſſe* has been fent with three *French-men*:
"*Yonnondio* not content with all this, has like-
"wife fent *Denneboot*," and two other *Mohawks*
"to perfwade us to meet him, and to fpeak
"with him of good Things. Should we not
"go to him, after all this Entreaty, when he
"is come fo far, and fo near to us, certainly
"if we did not, we fhould provoke his
"Wrath, and not deferve this Goodnefs. You
"fay we are Subjects to the King of *England*
"and *Duke of York*, but we fay, we are Bre-
"thren. We muft take care of our felves.
"Thofe Arms fixed upon the Poft without
"the Gate, cannot defend us againft the Arms
"of *La Barre*.

"*Brother Corlaer*, We tell you, That we
"fhall bind a Covenant Chain to our Arm,
"and to his, as thick as that Poft (*Pointing to
a Poft of the Houſe*) "Be not diſſatisfi'd; fhould
"we not imbrace this Happinefs offer'd to
"us, *viz*. Peace, in the plaee of War; yea,
"we fhall take the Evil doers, the *Sennekas* by
"the

Part I.   *Indian Nations.*   81

"the hand, and *La Barre* likewife, and their ax
"and his Sword fhall be thrown into a deep
"Water. We wifh our Brother *Corlaer*
"were prefent, but it feems the time will not
"permit of it.

Accordingly *Garangula*," one of the chief
Sachems of the *Onnondagas*, with thirty Warriors, went with Mr. *Le Maine* to meet the
Governor of *Canada* at *Kaihohage*. After he
had remain'd two Days in the *French* Camp
Mr. *La Barre* fpoke to him, as follows, (the
French Officers making a Semi-circle on one
fide while *Garangula*, with his Warriors, compleated the Circle on the other.)

(*b*) *Monf.* De La Barre's *Speech to* Garangula.

"THe King, my Mafter, being inform'd
"that the *Five Nations* have often infring'd
"the Peace, has order'd me to come hither
"with a Guard, and to fend *Ohqueffe* to the
"*Onnondagas* to bring the chief Sachems to
"my Camp. The Intention of the great
"King is, that you and I may fmoke the
"Calumet

(*b*) Voyages du Baron de la Hontan, Tome I. Lettre 7.

"Calumet (*c*) of Peace together, but on this Condition, that you Promise me, in the Name of the *Sennekas, Cayugas, Onnondagas, Oneydoes* and *Mohawks,* to give entire Satisfaction and Reparation to his Subjects, and for the future never to molest them.

"The *Sennekas, Cayugas, Onnondagas, Oneydoes* and *Mohawks* have Rob'd and Abus'd all the Traders that were passing towards the *Illinois* and *Umamies,* and other *Indian* Nations, the Children of my King. They have acted, on these occasions, contrary to the Treaty of Peace. with my Predecessor. I am order'd therefore to demand Satisfaction, and to tell them, That in case of of Refusal, or their Plundering us any more, that I have express Orders to declare War. *This Belt Confirms my Words.*

The

(*c*) The *Calumet* is a large Smoking Pipe, made of Marble, most commonly of a dark Red, well polished, shaped some-what in the form of a Hatchet, and adorned with large Feathers of several Colours. It is used in all the *Indian* Treatyes with Strangers, as a Flag of Truce between contending Partys, which all the *Indians* think a very high Crime to violate. These *Calumets* are generally of nice Workmanship, and were in use before the *Indians* knew any thing of the *Christians*; for which Reason we are at a loss to conceive by what means they pierced these Pipes and shaped them so finely, before they had the use of Iron.

"The Warriors of the *Five Nations* have conducted the *English* into the Lakes, which belong to the King, my Master, and brought the *English* among the Nations that are his Children, to destroy the Trade of his Subjects, and to with draw those Nations from him. They have carried the *English* thither notwithstanding the Prohibition of the late Governor of *New-York*, who fore-saw the Risque that both they and you would run. I am willing to forget these things, but if ever the like shall happen for the future, I have express Orders to declare War against you. *This Belt Confirms my Words.*

"Your Warriors have made several Barbarous Incursions on the *Ilinois* and *Umamies*. They have Massacreed Men, Women and Children, and have made many of these two Nations Prisoners, who thought themselves safe in their Villages, in time of Peace. These People, who are my Kings Children, must not be your Slaves, you must give them their Liberty, and send them back into their own Country. If the *Five Nations* shall refuse to do this, I have express Orders to declare War against them. *This Belt Confirms my Words.*

"This is what I had to say to *Garangula*, that he may carry to the *Sennekas, Cayugas, Onnondagas, Oneydoes* and *Mohawks* the Decla-

"ration which the King, my Master, has
"commanded me to make. He doth not
"wish them to force him to send a great Army
"to *Cadarackui Fort*, to begin a War, which
"must be fatal to them. He would be sorry
"that this Fort, which was the Work of
"Peace, should become the Prison of your
"Warriors. We must endeavour, on both sides,
"to prevent such Misfortunes. The *French*,
"who are the Brethren and Friends of the
"*Five Nations*, will never trouble their repose,
"Provided that the Satisfaction which I de-
"mand, be given, and that the Treatyes of
"Peace be hereafter observed. I shall be
"extreamly grieved if my words do not pro-
"duce the Effect which I expect from them;
"for then I shall be obliged to joyn with
"the Governor of *New-York*, who is
"Commanded by his Master to assist me, and
"burn the Castles of the *Five Nations*, and
"destroy you. *This Belt Confirms my Words.*"

Garangula was very much surprized to find the soft words of the *Jesuit*, and of the Governors Messengers, turn'd to such threatning Language. They were designed to strike Terror into the *Indians*. But *Garangula* having had good information, from those of the *Five Nations* living near *Cadarackui* Fort, of all the Sickness and other Misfortunes
which

which attended the *French* Army, they were far from producing the designed Effect. All the time that Monf. *De la Barre* spoke, *Garangula* kept his Eyes fixed upon the end of his Pipe. And as soon as the Governor had done speaking, he rose up, and having walked five or six times round the Circle, he returned to his place, where he spoke standing, while Monf. *De la Barre* kept his Elbow Chair, and said,

Garangula's *Answer*.

" YOnnondio, I Honour you, and the
" Warriors that are with me all likewise
" honour you. Your Interpreter has finished
" your Speech; I now begin mine. My
" words make haste to reach your Eears,
" hearken to them.

" *Yonnondio*, You must have believed when
" you left *Quebeck*, that the Sun had burnt up
" all the Forests which render our Country
" Unaccessible to the *French*, Or that the
" Lakes had so far overflown their Banks,
" that they had surrounded our Castles, and
" that it was impossible for us to get out of
" them. Yes, *Yonnondio*, surely you must have
" thought so, and the Curiosity of seeing so
" great a Country burnt up, or under Water,
" has brought you so far. Now you are
" undeceived, since that I and my Warriors
" are

" are come to assure you that the *Sennekas,*
" *Cayugas, Onnondagas, Oneydoes* and *Mohawks*
" are all alive. I thank you, in their Name,
" for bringing back into their Country the
" *Calumet* which your Predecessor received
" from their hands. It was happy for you
" that you left under ground that Murdering
" Hatchet which has been so often dyed in
" the Blood of the *French*. Hear *Yonnondio,*
" I do not Sleep, I have my eyes Open, and
" the Sun which enlightens me discovers to
" me a great Captain at the head of a Com-
" pany of Soldiers, who speaks as if he were
" Dreaming. He says that he only came to
" the Lake to smoke on the great *Calumet*
" with the *Onnondagas*. But *Garangula* says,
" that he sees the Contrary, that it was to
" knock them on the head, if Sickness had
" not weakned the Arms of the *French*.

" I see *Yonnondio* Raving in a Camp of
" sick men, who's Lives the great Spirit has
" saved, by Inflicting this Sickness on them.
" Hear *Yonnondio,* Our Women had taken
" their Clubs, our Children and Old Men
" had carried their Bows and Arrows into
" the heart of your Camp, if our Warriors
" had not disarmed them, and retained them
" when your Messenger, *Ohquesse* appeared
" in our Castle. It is done, and I have said it.

" Hear

"Hear *Yonnondio*, we plundered none of
" the *French*, but thofe that carried Guns,
" Powder and Ball to the *Twihties* and *Chic-*
" *taghicks*, becaufe thofe Arms might have
" coft us our Lives. Herein we follow the
" example of the Jefuits, who ftave all the
" Barrels of Rum brought to our Caftle,
" left the Drunken *Indians* fhould knock them
" on the Head. Our Warriors have not
" Bevers enough to pay for all thefe Arms
" that they have taken, and our Old Men are
" not afraid of the War. *This Belt pre-*
" *ferves my Words.*

" We carried the *Englifh* into our Lakes, to
" traffick there with the *Utawawas* and
" *Qutoghies*, as the *Adirondacks* brought the
" *French* to our Caftles, to carry on a Trade
" which the *Englifh* fay is theirs. We are
" born free, We neither depend upon *Yonnondio*
" nor *Corlaer*.

" We may go where we pleafe, and carry
" with us whom we pleafe, and buy and
" fell what we pleafe. If your Allies be your
" Slaves, ufe them as fuch, Command them
" to receive no other but your People. *This*
" *Belt Preferves my Words.*

" We knockt the *Twihtwies* and *Chictaghiks*
" on the head, becaufe they had cut down the
" Trees of Peace, which were the Limits of
" our Country. They have hunted Bevers
" on

" on our Lands: They have acted contrary
" to the Cuſtom of all *Indians*; for they left
" none of the Bevers alive, they kill'd both
" Male and Female. They brought the *Sa-*
" *tanas* (*d*) into their Country, to take part
" with them, and Arm'd them, after they had
" concerted ill Deſigns againſt us. We have
" done leſs than either the *Engliſh* or *French*,
" that have uſurp'd the Lands of ſo many
" *Indian* Nations, and chaſed them from their
" own Country. *This Belt Preſerves my*
" *Words*.

" Hear *Yonondio*, What I ſay is the Voice
" of all the *Five Nations*. Hear what they
" Anſwer, Open your Ears to what they
" Speak. The *Sennekas, Cayugas, Onnondagas,*
" *Oneydoes* and *Mohawks* ſay, That when they
" buried the Hatchet at *Cadarackui* (in the
" preſence of your Predeceſſor) in the middle
" of the Fort, they planted the Tree of
" Peace, in the ſame place, to be there care-
" fully preſerved, that, in place of a Retreat
" for Soldiers, that Fort might be a Rende-
" vouze of Merchants; that in place of Arms
" and Munitions of War, Bevers and Mer-
" chandize ſhould only enter there.

" Hear, *Yonondio*, Take care for the future,
" that ſo great a Number of Soldiers as ap-
" pear

(*d*) Called *Sawonons* by the *French*.

" pear here do not choak the Tree of Peace
" planted in fo fmall a Fort. It will be a great
" Lofs, if after it had fo eafily taken root,
" you fhould ftop its growth, and prevent its
" covering your Country and ours with its
" Branches. I affure you, in the Name of
" the *Five Nations*, That our Warriors fhall
" dance to the *Calumet of Peace* under its leaves,
" and fhall remain quiet on their Mats, and
" fhall never dig up the Hatchet till their
" Brethren, *Yonnondio* or *Corlaer* fhall either
" joyntly or feperately endeavour to attack
" the Country which the great Spirit has giv-
" en to our Anceftors. *This Belt preferves my*
" *Words, and this other, the Authority which the*
" Five Nations *have given me.*

Then *Garangula* addreffing himfelf to Mr. Le Main, faid,

" Take Courage, *Ohqueffe*, you have Spirit,
" Speak, Explain my Words, Forget no-
" thing, Tell all that your Brethren and
" Friends fay to *Yonnondio*, your Governor,
" by the Mouth of *Garangula*, who honours
" you, and defires you to accept of this Pre-
" fent of Bever, and take part with me in my
" Feaft, to which I invite you. This Prefent
" of Bevers is fent to *Yonnondio* on the part of
" the *Five Nations*."

When *Garangula*'s Harrangue was explain'd to

to Mr. *De la Barre*, he return'd to his Tent, enraged at what he had heard.

Garangula feasted the *French* Officers, and then Return'd. And Monf. *De la Barre* set out in in his way towards *Monreal*. As soon as the General was embarqued with the few Soldiers that remain'd in Health, the Militia made the best of their way to their own Habitations, without any Order or Discipline.

Thus a very Chargeable and Fatiguing Expedition (which was to strike the Terror of the *French* Name into the Stubborn Hearts of the *Five Nations*) ended by a Dispute between the *French* General and an Old *Indian*.

When the *Indians* came to *Albany*, after they had met with Mr. *De la Barre*, (and were upbraided for it by Coll. *Dongan*) *Carachkondie*,[42] an *Onnondaga*, flyly answer'd, *We are sorry, and ashamed; for now we understand that the Governor of* Canada *is not so great a Man as the* English *King that lives on the other side the great Water; and we are vexed for having given the Governor of* Canada *so many fine Wampum Belts.*

CHAP.

CHAP. V.

The English *Attempt to Trade in the Lakes, and* Mr. De Nonville *Attacks the* Sennekas.

MOnsieur *Le Marquis de Nonville* having succeeded Mr. *De la Barre*, in 1685. and having brought a confiderable Reinforcement of Soldiers with him, he resolv'd to Recover the Honour the *French* had lost in the last Expedition, and to Revenge the Slaughter that the *Five Nations* continued to make of the *Twihtwiks* and *Chictaghiks*, who had put themselves under the Protection of the *French*; for the *Five Nations* having entirely subdued the *Chicktaghiks*, (*e*) after a six years War, they resolv'd next to fall upon the *Twihtwies*, and to call them to an account for the Disturbance they had given some of the *Five Nations* in their Bever-hunting. The *Five Nations* have few or no Bevers in their own Country, and are for that reason obliged to hunt at a great distance, which often occasion'd Disputes with their Neighbours about the Property of the Bever, in some parts of the Country.

(*e*) Called *Ilinois* by the *French*.

The Bevers are the most valuable part of the *Indian* Trade. And as the *Twihtwies* carried their Bever to the *French*, the *English* favour'd the *Five Nations* in these Expeditions, and particularly in the beginning of the year 1687, made the *Five Nations* a Present of a Barrel of Powder, when their whole Force was preparing to go against the *Twihtwies*. The *English* were the better pleas'd with this War, because they thought it would divert their Thoughts from the *Indians* that were friends to *Virginia*:" But the *French* were resolv'd to Support their Friends more effectually by a powerful Diversion, and to change the Seat of the War.

For this purpose Mr. *De Nonville* sent, in *May*, 1687, great Quantities of Provisions to *Cadarackui* Fort, and gather'd the whole Force of *Canada* to *Montreal*. His Army consisted of 1500 *French* of the Regular Troops & Militia, and 500 *Indians* that lived near *Monreal* and *Quebeck*.

He sent likewise Orders to the Commandant at *Missilimakinak* to assemble all the Nations round him, and to March them to *Oniagara*, in order to joyn the Forces of *Canada* design'd against the *Sennekas*. And the other Officers posted among the *Indians* Westward, had the like Orders.

The *Twihtwies* receiv'd the Hatchet with joy, from the hands of the *French* Officer,
against

against the *Five Nations.* The *Outagamies* (*f*) *Kikabous,* and *Maskoutuhs,*" who were not us'd to Cannoes, were at first perswaded to joyn the *Twihtwies,* who were to march by Land to *Teuchsagrondie,* where there was a French Fort, at which they were to be supply'd with Ammunition: But after the *French* Officer left them, the *Utagamies* and *Maskuticks* were disswaded by some of the *Mahikander Indians,* who happen'd to be with a neighbouring Nation at that time.

The *Putewatemies, Malhominies* and *Puans* offer'd themselves willingly, and went to the Rendevouze at *Missilimakinak,* where they were receiv'd by the *Utawawas* with all the Marks of Honour usually paid to Soldiers, tho' the *Utawawas* had no inclination to the present Enterprize; they could not tell, however, how to appear against it, otherwise than by inventing what Delays they could to prevent their Marching."

In the mean while, a Cannoe arriv'd, which was sent by Mr. *De Nonville* with his Orders to the Officers. This Cannoe in her Passage discover'd some *English* commanded by Major *McGregory,* in their way to *Teiodondaraghie.* The *English* thought (after they had an account

---

(*f*) The *Outagamies, Kikabons, Malhominies* and *Puans* live on the West side of *Lake Michigan.*

of the new Alliance their King had enter'd into with the *French*) that the French would not disturb them in prosecuting a Trade with the Indians every where, and that the Trade would be equally free and open to both Nations. With these hopes a considerable Number of Adventurers, went out under the Conduct of Major *M‘ Gregory* to Trade with the Indians living on the Banks of the Lakes; and that they might be the more wellcome, perswaded the *Five Nations* to set all the *Dionondadie* Prisoners at Liberty, who went along with the *English* and conducted them towards *Missilimakinak* or *Teiodondoraghie*. But the *English* found themselves mistaken, for the *French* Commandant at *Teiodondoraghie*, as soon as he had Notice of this, sent 300 *French* to intercept the *English*."

(*g*) The *Utawawas* and *Dionondadies* having likewise an account of the *English*, designed to support their own Independency, and to encourage the *English* Trade. The Return of the *Dionondadie* Prisoners made that Nation very hearty in favouring the *English*, they therefore marched immediately off, with design to joyn Major *M‘ Gregory*, but

---

(*g*) Histoire de Le Amerique Septentrionale par Mr. De la Peterie, Tome 2. Chap. 16.

Part I.   *Indian Nations.*   95

the *Utawawas* were divided in their Inclinations, their Chief," with about thirty more joyn'd the *French*, the reft remain'd in fufpence and ftood Neuter.

The *Utawawas* thus wavering, difconcerted the Meafures of the *Deionondadies*, for they began to fufpect the *Utawawas*, and therefore immediately return'd to fecure their Wives and Children they had left near the *French* Fort with the *Utawawas*. The *Englifh* and their Effects were feized without any Oppofition, and were carried to the *French* fort at *Teiodondoraghie*.

The *Englifh* brought great Quantities of Rum with them, (which the *Indians* love more than their Life) and the *French* being afraid that if the *Indians* took to drinking, they would grow ungovernable, did what they could to keep them from it. They were moft concerned that the *Putewatemies*, (who had no knowledge of the *Englifh*, or of that bewitching Liquor, and were firmly attached to the *French*) fhould not tafte it.

The *Utawawas* ftill contrived delays to the March, and having got fome of the *Putewatemies* privately by themfelves, they offered them a Cag of Rum, and faid, "We are all "Bretheren, we ought to make one Body, "and to have one Soul. The *French* invite us "to War againft the *Five Nations*, with defign
                                                                          "to

" to make us Slaves, and that we should make
" our selves the Tools to effect it. As soon
" as they shall have destroyed the *Five Nations*,
" they will no longer observe any Measures
" with us, but use us like those Beasts that
" they tye to their Plows. Let us leave them
" to themselves, and they'll never be able to
" accomplish any thing against the *Five Na-*
" *tions*.

But the *Putewatemies* had entertain'd such Notions of the *French*, as made them Deaf to all the Politicks of the *Utawawas*."

The *French* however grew Jealous of these Caballings, and therefore resolv'd to delay their March no longer, and would not stay one day more for the *Utawawas*, who desired only so much time to Pitch their Canoes, but went away without them.

Mr. *Tonti* Commandant among the *Chictaghicks* met with another Party of the *English* of about 30 Men in *Lake Ohswego* as he marched with the *Chictaghicks* and *Twihtwiks*, and other neighbouring Nations to the General Rendevouze. He fell upon the *English*, Plundered them, and took them Prisoners.[68] The *French* divided all the Merchandize among the *Indians*, but kept the Rum to themselves and got all drunk. The *Deonondadie* Prisoners, that Conducted the *English*, joyned with the *Mihikander Indians* that were among Mr. *Tonti*'s
Indians

Indians (who had privately diffwaded about 200 of the neighbouring Nations from going along with *Tonti*) and endeavoured to perfwade all the *Indians* to fall upon the *French*, while they were drunk, and deftroy them, faying, *The* French *are a Proud, Imperious, Covetous People, that fell their goods at an extravagant Price*: *The* Englifh *are a good Natured, Honeft People, who will furnifh you with every thing at reafonable Rates*. But thefe arguments were to no purpofe, for thefe *far Indians* had entertained extraordinary Notions of the *French Power*, and knew nothing of the *Englifh*.

The *French* and *Putewatemies* being gone from *Teïodondoraghie*, the *Utawawas* began to be afraid of the *French* Refentment, and therefore the better to keep up the colour they had put on their delays, marched over Land with all poffible expedition, to the general Rendevouz near *Oniagara*, where all the *French* Force, both *Chriftian* and *Indian* was to meet."

The *Five Nations* being informed of the *French* Preparations, laid afide their Defigns againft the *Twihtwies*, and prepared to give the *French* a warm Reception. Upon this the Prieft at *Onnondaga*⁷⁰ left them, and their Soldiers came to *Albany* to provide Ammunition. The Commiffioners made them a Prefent of a confiderable quantity of Powder and Lead, befides what they purchafed. They were under

under a great deal of Concern when they took leave of the Commiffioners, and faid, " Since " we are to expect no other Affiftance from " our Brethren, we muft recommend our " Wives and Children to you, who will fly " to you, if any Misfortune fhall happen to " us. It may be we fhall never fee you more; " for we are refolved to behave fo as our " Brethren fhall have no reafon to be afha- " med of us."

We muft now return to Mr. *De Nonville*'s Army.

Monf. *Champigni* marched eight or ten Days before the reft of the Army, with between two and three hundred *Canadiens*. As foon as they arriv'd at *Cadarackui*, they furprized two Villages of the *Five Nations*, that were fettled about eight Leagues from that Place, to prevent their giving any intelligence to their own Nation of the *French* Preparations, or the State of the *French* Army, as it was fuppofed they did in the laft Expedition under Mr. *De la Barre*. Thefe People were furprifed when they leaft expected, and by them from whom they fear'd no harm, becaufe they had fettled there at the Invitation and on the Faith of the *French*. They were carried in cold Blood to the Fort, and tyed to Stakes to be tormented

by

by the *French Indians* (*Chriſtians*, as they call them) while they continued ſinging in their Country manner, and upbraiding the *French* with their Perfidy and Ungratitude. But the *French* Policy had no Compaſſion on theſe Miſerable People, when they were reſolved to deſtroy their whole Nation."

While Mr. *De Nonville* was at *Cadarackui* Fort, he had an Account that the *Chicktaghiks* and *Twihtwies* waited for the *Quatoghies* and *Utawawas* at (*h*) *Lake St. Clair*, with whom they deſign'd to March to the general Rendevouz at the Mouth of the *Sennekas River*. For this Expedition was chiefly deſign'd againſt the *Sennekas*, who had abſolutely refuſed to meet Mr. *De la Barre*, and were moſt firmly attached to the *Engliſh*. The *Sennekas* for this reaſon were deſign'd to be made Examples of the *French* Reſentment to all the other Nations of *Indians*.

The Meſſenger having aſſured the General, that it was time to depart, in order to meet the Weſtern *Indians*, that came to his Aſſiſtance, he ſet out the 23d of *June*, and ſent one part of his Army in Canoes, along the North Shoar, while he with the other part paſſed along the South, that no accidents of wind

---

(*b*) In the Streights between *Oſſwego Lake* and *Quatoghie Lake*,

might prevent the one or the other reaching within the time appointed at the Place the *Indians* were to meet him. It happened, by reason of the good weather that both the Parties arrived on the same day, and joyned the Western *Indians* at *Irondequat*.¹³ As soon as the men were put on shoar, they hawled up the Canoes, and began a Fort, where 400 Men were left to guard the Canoes, and the Baggage. Here a young *Canadien* was shot to death, as a Deserter, for conducting the *English* into the Lakes, tho' the two Nations were not only at Peace, but their Kings in stricter Friendship than usual. But this Piece of severity is not to be wonder'd at, when the *French* were resolved to undertake an unjust War, and every thing to put a stop to the *English* Trade, which now began to extend it self far into the Continent, and would in its consequence ruin theirs. The next day the Army began to march towards the chief Village of the *Sennekas*, which was only seven Leagues distant, every man carrying ten Biskets for his Provision. The *Indian* Traders made the Van with part of the *Indians*, the other part marched in the Rear, while the Regular Troops and Militia compos'd the main Body.* The Army marched four Leagues the first day, without discovering any thing. The next day the scouts advanced before the Army, as far as the corn Fields of the

Indian Nations.

the Village, without feeing any body, tho' they paffed within Piftol fhot of 500 *Sennekas*, that lay on their Bellies, and let them pafs and repafs, without difturbing them.

On the Report which they made, the *French* Marched with much hafte, but little Order, in hopes to overtake the Women, Children and Old Men; for they no longer doubted of all being fled. But as foon as the *French* reached the foot of a Hill, about a quarter of a League from the Village, the *Sennekas* suddenly rais'd the War-fhout, with a Difcharge of their Fire-Arms. This put the Regular Troops, as well as the Militia into fuch a Fright, as they marched through the Woods, that the Battalions immediately divided, and run to the Right and Left, and in the Confufion fired upon one another. When the *Sennekas* perceived their Diforder, they fell in among them Pell-mell, till the *French Indians*, more ufed to fuch Fights, gathered together and Repulfed the *Sennekas*. There were (according to the *French* Accounts) a hundred *French-men*, ten *French Indians*, and about fourfcore *Sennekas* kill'd in this Rencounter.

Mr. *De Nonvelle* was fo dif-fpirited with the Fright that his Men had been put into, that his *Indians* could not perfwade him to purfue. He halted the remainder of that Day. The next day he Marched on with defign to burn

the

the Village, but when he came there, he found the *Sennekas* had faved him the trouble; for they had laid all in Afhes before they Retired; Two Old Men only were found in the Caftle, who were cut into Pieces and boyled to make Soop for the *French* Allies. The *French* ftaid five or fix Days to deftroy their Corn, and then marched to two other Villages, at two or three Leagues diftance. After they had perform'd the like Exploits in thofe Places they return'd to the Banks of the Lake."

Before the *French* left the Lakes, they built a Fort of four Baftions at *Oniagara*, on the South fide of the Streights, between *Ohfwego Lake* and *Cadarackui Lake*, and left a hundred Men, with eight Months Provifions in it. But this Garrifon was fo clofely blockt up by the *Five Nations*, that they all dy'd of Hunger, except feven or eight, who were accidentally reliev'd by a Party of *French Indians*."

The *Weftern Indians* when they parted from the *French* General, made their Harrangues, as ufual, in which they told him with what Pleafure they faw a Fort fo well placed to favour their Defigns againft the *Five Nations*, and that they Relied on his never Finifhing the War but with the Deftruction of the *Five Nations*, or Forceing them to abandon their Country. He affured them, that he would act with fuch
Vigour

Vigour that they would foon fee the *Five Nations* driven into the Sea.

He fent a Detachment of Soldiers to *Teiodondoraghie*, and in his Return to *Canada*, which was by the North fide of the Lake, he left the fame Number of Men and Quantity of Provifions at *Cadarackui* Fort.

The *French* having got nothing but dry Blows, fent thirteen of the *Indians* that they furprized at *Cadarackui*, to *France*, as Trophies of their Victory, where they were put into the Galleys, as Rebels to their King."

CHAP. VI.

Coll. Dongan's *Advice to the* Indians. Adario's *Enterprize, and* Montreal *Sacked by the* Five Nations.

COll. *Dongan,* who always had the *Indian Affairs* very much at heart, met the *Five Nations* at *Albany* as foon as poffible after the *French* Expedition, and fpoke to them on the 5th of *Auguft*, in the following words, *viz.*

Brethren;

" I Am very glad to fee you here in this
" Houfe, and am heartily glad that you
" have

" have fuſtain'd no greater loſs by the *French*,
" tho' I believe it was their Intention to de-
" ſtroy you all, if they could have ſurpriz'd
" you in your Caſtles.

" As ſoon as I heard of their defin to War
" with you, I gave you Notice, and came up
" hither my ſelf, that I might be ready to give
" all the Aſſiſtance and Advice that ſo ſhort a
" time would allow me.

" I am now about ſending a Gentleman to
" *England*, to the King, my Maſter, to let
" him know, that the *French* have invaded
" his Territories on this ſide the great
" Lake, and War'd upon the Brethren, his
" Subjects. I would therefore willingly
" know, whether the Brethren have given
" the Governor of *Canada* any Provocation
" or not; and if they have, how, and in what
" manner, becauſe I am oblig'd to give a
" true account of this matter. This buſineſs
" may cauſe a War between the King of
" *England* and the *French* King, both in *Europe*
" and here, and therefore I muſt know the
" Truth.

I know the Governor of *Cananda* dare not
" enter into the great King of *England*'s
" Territories, in a Hoſtile manner, without
" Provocation, if he thought the Brethren
" were the King of *England*'s Subjects; But
" you having two or three years ago, made a
" Covenant

"Covenant Chain with the *French*, contrary
"to my Command, (which I knew could
"not hold long) being void of it felf among
"the *Chriſtians*; for as much as Subjects (as
"you are) ought not to treat with any Fo-
"reign Nation," it not lying in your Power,
"have brought this Trouble upon your felves,
"and, as I believe, is the only reafon of their
"falling upon you at this time.

"*Brethren*, I took it very ill, that after you
"had put your felves into the Number of
"the great King of *England*'s Subjects, that
"you fhould ever offer to make Peace or
"War without my confent. You know that
"we can live without you, but you cannot
"live without us. You never found that I
"told you a Lie, and I did offer you Affift-
"ance as you wanted, provided that you
"would be advifed by me; for I know the
"*French* better than any of you do.

"Now fince there is a War begun upon
"you by the Governor of *Canada*, I hope
"without any Provocation by you given," I
"defire and command you, that you hearken
"to no Treaty but by my Advice, which if
"you follow, you fhall have the Benefit of
"the great Chain of Friendfhip between the
"great King of *England* and the *French* King,
"which came out of *England* the other day,
"and which I have fent to *Canada* by *Anthony*

" *Le Junard*;" In the mean time I will give
" you such Advice as will be for your good,
" and will supply you with such Necessarys
" as you will have need of.

" *First*, My Advice is, that as many Pri-
" soners of the *French*, as you shall take, that
" you draw not their Blood, but bring them
" home and keep them to Exchange for your
" People, which they have Prisoners already
" or may take hereafter.

" 2*dly*, That if it be Possible, that you can
"order it so, I would have you take one or
" two of your wisest Sachems, and one or
" two chief Captains of each Nation, to be
" a Council to manage all Affairs of the War.
" They to give Orders to the rest of the
" Officers what they are to do, that your
" designs may be kept Private, for after it
" comes among so many People, it is Blazed
" abroad, and your designs are often frustrated.
" And those chief Men to keep a Corre-
" spondence with me, by a Trusty Messen-
" ger.

" 3*dly*, Now the Great matter under
" Consideration with the Brethren, is, how
" to strengthen themselves, and weaken your
" Enemy. My Opinion is, that the Brethren
" should send Messengers to the *Utawawas*,
" *Twihtwichs*, and the farther *Indians*, and to
" send back likewise some of the Prisoners of
" these

" thefe Nations, if any you have left, to
" bury the Hatchet, and to make a Covenant
" Chain, that they may put away all the
" *French* that are among them, and that you
" will open a Path for them this way. They
" being the King of *England*'s Subjects like-
" wife, only the *French* have been admitted to
" Trade with them, for all that the *French* have
" in *Canada*, they had it of the Great King of
" *England*, that by that Means they may come
" hither freely where they may have every
" thing Cheaper than among the *French*.
" That you and they may joyn together againſt
" the *French*, and make ſo firm a League that
" whoever is an Enemy to one, muſt be to
" both.

" 4*thly*, Another thing of Concern is, that
" you ought to do what you can to open a
" Path for all the *North Indians* and *Mahikanders*
" that are among the *Utawawas* and farther
" Nations: I will endeavour to do the ſame,
" to bring them home; for they not daring
" to return home your way, the *French* keep
" them there on purpoſe to joyn with the
" farther Nations againſt you, for your Deſtru-
" ction; for you know, that one of them is
" worſe than ſix of the others. Therefore all
" means muſt be uſed to bring them Home,
" and uſe them kindly as they paſs through
" your Country.

5thly,

" 5*thly*, My Advice further is, That Mef-
" fengers go in behalf of all the *Five Nations*,
" to the *Christian Indians* at *Canada*,
" to perfwade them to come Home to their
" Native Country, and to promife them
" all Protection. This will be another great
" means to weaken your Enemy; but if they
" will not be advifed, you know what to do
" with them."

" 6*thly*, I think it very neceffary for the
" Brethrens Security and Affiftance, and to
" the endamaging the *French*, to build a Fort
" upon the Lake, where I may keep Stores
" and Provifions in cafe of neceffity; and
" therefore I would have the Brethren let me
" know what Place will be moft convenient
" for it.

" 7*thly*, I would not have the Brethren keep
" their Corn in their Caftles, as I hear the
" *Onnondagas* do, but to bury it a great way in
" the Woods, where few People may know
" where it is, for fear of fuch an Accident as
" has happen'd to the *Sennekas*.

" 8*thly*, I have given my Advice in your
" General Affembly by Mr. *Dirk Weffels* and
" *Akus* the Interpreter, how you are to manage
" your Partys, and how neceffary it is to get
" Prifoners, to exchange for your own Men
" that are Prifoners with *t*he *French*. And I
" am glad to hear that the Brethren are fo
" United, as Mr. *Dirk Weffels* tells me you
                                              " are

Part I. *Indian Nations.*

" are, and that there are no Rotten Members
" nor *French* Spyes among you.

" 9*thly*, The Brethren may remember my
" Advice which I fent you this Spring, Not
" to go to *Cadarackui* ; if you had, they would
" have ferv'd you as they did your People
" who came from Hunting thither; for I
" told you then, that I knew the *French* better
" than you did.

" 10*thly*. There was no Advice or Propo-
" fition that I made to the Brethren, all the
" time that the Prieft liv'd at *Onondaga*, but
" what he wrote to *Canada*, as I found by one
" of his Letters, which he gave to an Indian
" to carry to *Canada*, but was brought hither.
" Therefore I defire the Brethren not to re-
" ceive him or any *French Priefts* any more,
" having fent for *Englifh Priefts*, with whom
" you may be fupply'd to your Content."

" 11. I would have the Brethren look out
" fharp for fear of being furprifed. I be-
" lieve all the Strength of the *French* will be
" at their Frontier Places, *viz.* at *Cadarackui*
" and *Oniagara*, where they build a Fort now,
" and at *Trois Rivieres, Montreal* and *Chambly*.

" 12. Let me put you in mind again, not
" to make any Treatys without my Means,
" which will be more Advantagious for you,
" than your doing it by your felves, for then
" you will be look'd upon as the King of
" *England*'s

"England's Subjects. And let me know, from
"time to time, every thing that is done.

"Thus far I have spoken to you relating to
"the War.

Then he chid them for their Breach of Faith
with *Virginia*. He told them, that he was inform'd that laſt Spring they had kill'd a fine Gentleman, with ſome others, and that a Party of the *Oneydoes* was now there at the head of *James" River*, with intention to deſtroy all the *Indians* there-about. They had taken ſix Priſoners, whom he order'd them to bring to him, to be Reſtored; and that for the future they ſhould deſiſt from doing any Injury to the People of *Virginia* or their *Indians*, otherwiſe all the *Engliſh* would unite to deſtroy them. But at the ſame time he free'd the *Sennekas* from any blame, and commended them as a *brave and honeſt People, who never had done any thing contrary to his Orders,* except in making that unlucky Peace with the French *three years a go.*

Laſtly, He recommended to them, Not to ſuffer their People to be Drunk, during the War: A Soldier thereby (he ſaid) looſes his Reputation, becauſe of the Advantages it will give the Enemy over him.

This honeſt Gentleman earneſtly purſued the Intereſt of his Country; but, it ſeems, his Meaſures were not agreeable to thoſe his
Maſter

Master had taken with the *French* King; for he had Orders to procure a Peace for the *French*, and was soon after this Removed from his Government. Indeed such an Active, as well as Prudent Governor of *New-York*, could not be acceptable to the *French*, who had the Universal Monarchy in view, in *America* as well as in *Europe*.

Coll. *Dongan*'s Message to Mr. *De Nonville* at a time when the Crowns of *England* and *France* had so lately entred into a strict Friendship, had, no doubt, some Influence on the *French* Governor. But the little Success he had in his Expensive and Dangerous Expedition, together with the Obstruction that the *French* Trade met with from the War, inclin'd him more effectually to Proposals of Peace, which Coll. *Dongan* was forced to make, and the *Five Nations* to yield to: For notwithstanding Coll. *Dongan*'s Advice to them, as above related, he by his Masters Orders (who was entirely devoted to Bigotry and the *French* Interest) obliged the *Five Nations* to agree to a Cessation of Arms, and to deliver up their Prisoners without any Conditions, in order to obtain a Peace on such Terms as the *French* should agree to. And that no Accident might prevent, Mr. *De Nonville* sent his Orders to all his Officers in the *Indian* Countrys to observe a Cessation of Arms till the Ambassadors of the

Five

Five Nations should meet him at *Montreal*, as they had given him reason to expect in a little time, to conclude the Peace in the usual Form."

In the mean time, *Adario*, the chief of the *Deonondadies*, finding that his Nation was become suspected by the *French*, since the time they had shown so much Inclination to the *English* when they attempted to Trade at *Missilimakinak*, Resolved by some brave Action against the *Five Nations* to recover the good Graces of the *French*.

For this Purpose he Marched from *Missilimakinak* at the head of a hundred Men; and that he might act with more Security, he took *Cadarackui* Fort in his way for Intelligence: The Commandant informed him, that Mr. *De Nonville* was in hopes of concluding a Peace with the *Five Nations*, and expected their Embassadors in eight or ten days at *Montreal* for that purpose, and therefore desired him to return to *Missilimakinak* without attempting any thing that might Obstruct so good a Design.

The *Indian* being surprized with this News, was under great Concern for his Nation, which he was afraid would be sacrificed to the *French* Resentment or Interest, but dissembled his Concern before the *French* Officer. He went from *Cadarackui*, not to return home as the Commandant thought, but to wait for the

the *Ambaſſadors* of the 5 *Nations* near one of the Falls of *Cadarackui River*, by which he knew they muſt paſs. He did not lurk there above four or five days before the unhappy Deputies came guarded by forty young Soldiers, who were all ſurpriſed & kill'd or taken Priſoners. As ſoon as the Priſoners were all ſecured, the cunning *Deonondadie* told them " That he having
" been enformed by the Governor of *Canada*,
" That Fifty Warriors of their Nation were
" to paſs this way about this time, he had
" ſecured this Paſs, not doubting of inter-
" cepting them.

The Ambaſſadors being much ſurpris'd with the *French* Perfidy, told *Adario* the Deſign of their Journey, who, the better to play his part, ſeem'd to grow Mad and Furious, declaiming againſt Mr. *De Nonville*, and ſaid, *He would, ſome Time or other be Revenged of him for making a Tool of him to commit ſuch horrid Treachery.* Then looking ſtedfaſtly on the Priſoners (among whom *Dekaneſora* was the Principal Ambaſſador) *Adario* ſaid to them, *Go my Brethren, I Unty your Bonds, and ſend you Home again, tho' our Nations be at War;* The French *Governor has made me commit ſo black an Action, that I ſhall never be eaſy after it till your* Five Nations *ſhall have taken full Vengeance.*

This was ſufficient to perſwade the Ambaſſadors of the Truth of what he ſaid, who assured him, That he and his Nation might make their Peace when they pleased. *Adario* lost only one Man on this occasion, and would keep a *Satana* Slave, (adopted into the *Five Nations*) to fill up his place. Then he gave Arms, Powder and Ball to the rest of the Prisoners, to enable them to Return.

The Ambassadors were chiefly if not all, *Onnondagas* and *Oneydoes*, who had been long under the influence of the *French Priests*, and still retain'd an Affection to them; but this Adventure throughly changed their thoughts, and irritated them so heartily against the *French*, that all the *Five Nations* from this time prosecuted the War unanimously.

Adario deliver'd the Slave (his Prisoner) to the *French* at *Missilimakinak*, who to keep up the Enmity between the *Deonondadies* and the *Five Nations*, order'd him to be shot to Death. As they carried him out, he related the whole of the Action, but the *French* thinking that he had only contrived it to save his Life, had no regard to it, till the fatal Consequences call'd his Dying Words to their Remembrance, with sorrowful Reflections.

The same Day that the *Satana* was shot, *Adario* call'd one of the *Five Nations*, who had been long a Prisoner, to be an Eye-witness of his Country-mans Death, then bid him make his Escape to his own Country, to give an
Account

Account of the *French* Cruelty, from which it was not in his Power to fave a Prifoner he himfelf had taken."

This heighten'd the Rage of the *Five Nations*, fo that Mr. *De Nonville*'s fending to difown *Adario* (*m*) in this Action, had no effect upon them: Their Breafts admitted of no thought but that of R e v e n g e. It was not not long before the *French* felt the Bloody effects of this cruel Paffion; for 1200 Men of the *Five Nations* invaded the ifland of *Montreal* when the *French* had no fufpicion of any fuch Attempt, while Mr. *De Nonville* and his Lady were in that Town. They Landed on the fouth fide of the Ifland at *La Chine*, on the 26*th* of *July*, 1688. where they burnt and facked all the Plantations, and made a terrible Maffacre of Men, Women and Children. The *French* were under apprehenfion of the Town's being attacked, for which reafon they durft not fend out any confiderable Party to the Relief of the Country, till the *Indians* had blocked up two Forts, when Mr. *De Nonville* fent out a hundred Soldiers and fifty *Indians* to try to bring off the men, The *French* of this Party were all either taken or cut to pieces, except one Soldier and the Commanding Officer, who was carried off by twelve *Indians* that made their efcape, after he had his Thigh broke. There was above a Thousand of the *French* kill'd at this time, and Twenty six were carried away Prisoners, the greatest part of which were burnt alive. The *Five Nations* only lost three Men in this Expedition, that got Drunk, and were left behind. This, however, did not satiate their Thirst after Blood; for in *October* following they destroy'd likewise all the lower part of the Island, and carried away many Prisoners."

The Consequences of these Expeditions were very dismal to the *French*, for they were forced to burn their two Barks which they had on *Cadarackui Lake*, and to abandon their Fort there. They design'd to have blown up their Works when they left that place, and for that end left a lighted Match where the Powder lay, but were in such a Fright, that they durst not stay to see what effect it had. They went down *Cadarackui River*, in seven Birch Canoes, and for greater Security travel'd in the Night. One of the Canoes with all the men in it was lost by their Precipitation, as they passed one of the Falls of that River. The *Five Nations* hearing that the *French* had deserted *Cadarackui* Fort, 50 *Indians* went and took Possession of it, who found the Match the *French* had left, which had gone out, and 28 Barrils of Powder in the same place, together with several other Stores."

The News of the Success the *Five Nations* had

had over the *French*, soon spread itself among all the *Indians*, and put the *French* Affairs every where into terrible Disorder.

The *Utawawas* had always shown an Inclination to the *English*, and they therefore immediately sent openly four Sachems with three Prisoners of the *Sennekas* that they had, to assure them, That they would forever Renounce all Friendship with the *French*, and promised to Restore the rest of the Prisoners. They also included seven Nations that liv'd near *Missilimakinak*, in this Peace.

This put the *French* commandant there under the greatest Difficulty to maintain his Post; but there was no Choice, he must stand his Ground; for the *Five Nations* had cut off all hopes of Retiring.

The *Nepeciriniens* and *Kikabous*, of all their Numerous Allies, only remain'd firm to the *French*, every one of the others endeavour'd to gain the Friendship of the 5 *Nations*, and would certainly have done it, by Massacreing all the *French* among them, if the Sieur *Perot* had not with wonderful Sagacity and imminent Hazard to his own Person diverted them, for which *Canada* cannot do too much Honour to that Gentlemans Memory."

Canada was now in a most Miserable Condition; for while the greatest Number of their Men had been employ'd in the Expeditions against

againſt the *Five Nations*, and in Trading among the *far Nations*, and making New Diſcoveries and Settlements, Tillage and Huſbandry had been neglected; now they loſt ſeveral Thouſands of their Inhabitants by the continual Incurſions of ſmall Parties, ſo that none durſt hazard themſelves out of the Fortified Places. Indeed, it is not eaſie to conceive what Diſtreſs the *French* were then under; for tho' they were almoſt every where ſtarving, they could not Plant nor Sow, or go from one Village to another for Relief, but with imminent Danger of having their Scalps carried away by the Sculking *Indians*. At laſt the whole Country being laid Waſte, Famine began to rage, and was like to have put a Miſerable End to that Colony.

If the *Indians* had underſtood the method of attacking Forts, nothing could have preſerved the *French* from an entire Deſtruction at this time. For whoever conſiders the ſtate of the *Indian* Affairs during this Period, How the *Five Nations* were divided in their Sentiements and Meaſures; The *Onnondagas*, *Cayugas*, and *Oneydoes*, under the Influence of the *French* Jeſuits, were diverted from proſecuting the War with *Canada*, by the Jeſuits cunningly ſpiriting up thoſe three Nations againſt the *Virginia Indians*, and perſwading them to ſend out their Parties that way

way: The *Sennekas* had a War at the fame time upon their hands with three numerous *Indian Nations*, the *Utawawas, Chicktaghicks* and *Twihtwies*: And the Meafures the *Englifh* obferved with the *French* all King *James*'s Reign, gave the *Indians* rather grounds of Jealoufy than Affiftance. I fay, whoever confiders all thefe things, and what the *Five Nations* did actually perform under all thefe Difadvantages againft the *French*, will hardly doubt that the *Five Nations* by themfelves were at that time an over Match for the *French* of C A N A D A.

The End of the Firft Part.

NOTES.

(1) WILLIAM BURNET, the Governor to whom Dr. Colden dedicates his hiſtory, and within whoſe province it was written and publiſhed, was a ſon of the famous Biſhop of Saliſbury.

He had been Comptroller of the Cuſtoms in London, a poſt worth £1,200 per annum, but loſing heavily in South Sea ſpeculations, effected a ſort of exchange with Governor Hunter, hoping to retrieve his fortunes in America.

He was appointed Governor of New York and New Jerſey in April, 1720 (N. Y. Col. Doc. v. 586), and publiſhed his Commiſſion in New York September 17, and at North Amboy, N. J., September 22.

He at once became popular by his manners. "A man of ſenſe and polite breeding," ſays Smith, "a well-read ſcholar, ſprightly and of a ſocial diſpoſition. Being devoted to his books he abſtained from all thoſe exceſſes into which his pleaſurable reliſh would otherwiſe have plunged him. He ſtudied the arts of recommending himſelf to the people, had nothing of the moroſeneſs of a ſcholar, was gay and condeſcending, affected no pomp, but viſited every family of reputation, and often diverted himſelf in free converſe with the ladies."

He ſeems, indeed, to have found New York ſociety and ladies ſo pleaſing that before he had been a year inſtalled

inſtalled he married Anna Maria, daughter of Abraham Van Horn, an eminent merchant and ſubſequently member of the Colonial Council.

As a Governor he was one of the beſt that ever viſited New York in colonial times. To limit the power of the French on the North and Weſt he ſaw to be eſſential to the wealth and progreſs of New York. The French in Canada poſſeſſed great influence at the Weſt through their extenſive trade, the goods being, however, frequently Engliſh fabrics furniſhed from the colony of New York. Burnet ſought to break up this trade, and direct the energies of New York to the opening of direct channels of commerce with the Weſtern Indians. With this view he erected a trading poſt at Oſwego in 1722, attracted the Weſtern tribes to join the Five Nations, exerted himſelf to defeat the French in their project of a fort at Niagara, and finally, in 1727, replaced his trading houſe at Oſwego by a fort.

"The exceſſive love of money, a diſeaſe common to all his Predeceſſors, and to ſome who ſucceeded him," ſays Smith, "was a vice from which he was entirely free. He ſold no offices, nor attempted to raiſe a fortune by indirect means; for he lived generouſly, and carried ſcarce anything away with him but his books. Theſe were to him inexhauſtible ſources of delight. His aſtronomical obſervations have been uſeful; but by his Comment on the *Apocalypſe* he expoſed himſelf, as other learned men have before him, to the criticiſms of thoſe who have not ability to write half ſo well."—(Hiſt. Province of New York. London, 1757, pp. 172–3.)

He was ſuperſeded by the appointment of John Montgomery, Eſq., Governor of New York, Auguſt 12,

12, 1727 (N. Y. Col. Doc. v. 823), and delivered the great feals to that gentleman April 15, 1728.

His removal from this congenial pofition was not his only affliction: about the fame time he loft his wife, and, thus bereaved and difappointed, proceeded to Bofton to affume the difficult poft of Governor of Maffachufetts. "His fuperior talents and free and eafy manner of communicating his fentiments made him the delight of men of fenfe and learning," fays Mr. Hutchinfon (Hift. of Maffachufetts, vol. ii. ch. 3); but this was not enough. His fhort career in Maffachufetts was as unpleafant as that in New York had been agreeable. A long ftruggle with the General Court embittered his days, and the excitement produced upon him feems to have undermined his health. After adjourning the Court to meet in Cambridge in Auguft, 1729, he fell fick at Bofton, and died September 7, 1729. The Court which refufed him a falary gave him a pompous funeral.

His iffue by his firft wife feems to have been one fon, Gilbert; by Mifs Van Horn he had William and Thomas, a daughter, Mary, who married Hon. William Brown, of Beverley, Mafs., and a child who died young.

His will, dated New York, September 6, 1727, alludes to his wife as dead; it was proved at Bofton, September 25, 1729, his property amounting only to £4,540 4s. 3½d.

A correfpondent of the Hiftorical Magazine (vol. viii, p. 398) ftates that he has two manufcript fermons—that preached in the chapel of the fort of New York on the interment of Mrs. Burnet, by Rev. Mr. Orum, unfortunately not dated, and that preached at the Governor's funeral in "the King's Chapple

Chapple, in Boston, in New England, the 12th day of September, in the year 1729, by the Rev. Mr. Price."

(2) Canada.

(3) See Edition of 1747 (8vo, London), pp. 136, 186, 191, &c.

(4) It is not easy to say what French works are here alluded to, probably Hennepin and La Hontan. Of other French works bearing on Iroquois history, Colden appears to have seen only de la Potherie. Champlain, the Jesuit Relations, Lafitau, and the Lettres Edifiantes were probably inaccessible at the time to one writing, as he did, at New York. But it is strange to see how completely, sixty years after the English occupancy, the sixty years of Dutch rule, with all the writings of that period, were despised and ignored. The tract of Megapolensis on the Indians, the works of Van Der Donck and De Vries, which would have given him much, are all overlooked. The only special English works on New York published prior to Colden's work, Denton, Woolley, Miller, give little direct information as to the Five Nations, and we can scarcely wonder at all absence of allusion to them.

(5) Dr. Colden should have taken better care of these "Minutes of the Commissioners of Indian Affairs." He appreciated their value, but finding them in a wretched condition, left them so, subject to utter loss. Fortunately, in 1751, Mr. Alexander (thank him, all ye antiquaries of New York) " borrowing them for his perusal, had them bound up in four

four large volumes in folio."—(Smith's Hiftory of New York, p. 154, note.)

(6) European nations, as relics identical with thofe of America fhow, had their ftone and their copper age before reaching that when iron made progrefs rapid. Our Northern Indians were ftill in the ftone age, Mexico and Peru had reached that of copper.

(7) Hence a report of a fpeech of an educated French interpreter, fully converfant with the language, as miffionary or agent, would feem to be more truftworthy.

(8) The names of tribes and places here given fuggeft fome curious reflections. Neither Englifh nor French names have prevailed exclufively. We have adopted the French terms Abenaki, Algonquin, Chicago, Detroit, Huron, Illinois, Iroquois, Lake Huron, Miami, Michilimackinac, Lake Ontario, Shawnee, here treated as words fo foreign to our fathers as to need explanation. One name, Illinois, was as new to Wafhington when he wrote his firft diary, for, not catching it clearly, he made it out *Ifles Noires*, and tranflates it *Black Iflands*—little forefeeing his own future or his country's ; little dreaming that he was to be the firft Prefident of a great Republic, and that that Illinois would one day fend, as his fucceffor in the city of his name, in his hold on the affections of the people, a grandfon of one of the backwoodfmen of his own Virginia. A few remarks will here be made on thefe names.

ADIRONDACKS means tree-eaters.—(See Hiftorical Magazine, vol. iv. p. 185.)

AMIHOUIS

AMIHOUIS is probably meant for *Amikoues*, the Beaver Indians; but it is an error to make the French call the Tionontates by the name. They called them at firſt Petun or Tobacco Indians, and after their great defeat and flight Hurons. They now go by the name of Wyandots, although they are a diſtinct tribe from them.—(See Hiſtorical Magazine, vol. v. p. 262.)

ANIEZ Colden here makes a kind of bull. The word Aniez, though given as the name which the Five Nations did *not* give the Mohawks, is really the name they did give—Gagniegue*baga* or Gagniegue*ronon*, the termination meaning people. Mohawk is from Maqua, the Mohegan name for bear, the name of the tribe as a body.

HURONS. The name Quatoghie occurs very rarely except in Colden. In the whole courſe of the Colonial Documents Dr. O'Callaghan gives but two references to this name in his index. The tribe called themſelves Wendat (Relation de la Nouv. France, 1639, p. 50; 1640, p. 35), whence the more common Engliſh name Wyandot was formed. Huron was merely a French nickname.

LOUPS is a French tranſlation of the Algic word Maikan or Mohegan, a wolf. The Mohawks called them, and ſtill call the Stockbridge Indians, Agotſagenens.

MASCOUTENS, Odiſtagheks. The Hurons called them Aſſiſtague or Fire Indians.

ONNONTIO, YONNONDIO, means Great Mountain, and is ſimply an Indian tranſlation of the name of Montmagny (Mons Magnus),

Notes. 127

Magnus), the second Governor of Canada, retained as a title, just as Arendt Van Curler's name, reduced to Corlar, was used by the Iroquois to mean the Governor of the Dutch or English at New York.

OUTAGAMI is the proper name of the Foxes, whom Colden makes to be the Quaksies of the Iroquois; the Scunksiks being apparently the Sacs.

OTTAWAS. The French give Ontwagannha and Twakanna as the Iroquois name of this tribe.

TATERAS, TODERIKS, are the Catawbas.

TONGORIAS appears on one of De Lisle's maps as the name of a tribe on the Tennessee; I find no other French allusion to the name. The Toteros, who have given the name of Totteroy to Great Sandy Creek, may be the same. (N. Y. Col. Doc. III, 194, n.) Colden's English seems to make them the Erié, e of the Hurons, the Eriégue, Erique of the Iroquois.

(9) This statement, supported by later authorities, is omitted in the English edition.—(See Morgan's League of the Iroquois, p. 96.)

(10) The whole question of the families or tribes is discussed in Morgan's League of the Iroquois (Rochester, 1851, 8vo), chapter iv. The Mohawks and Oneidas had but these three tribes, as all writers, French and English, declare, but the other nations, according to Morgan, had generally eight.

(11)

(11) The Sachems, fifty in all, were the heads of the families, and used the mark of the animal whose name they bore in signing treaties. The rank was not hereditary from father to son—indeed, a Sachem's son could scarcely be a Sachem. A man could not marry in his own family, and the children belonged to the mother's, not to the father's, family. When a Sachem died, the family chose as his successor, or tacitly admitted, the succession of a uterine brother, or a sister's son, or some more distant relative of the same family, and consequently related only in the female line to the deceased. This explains how some have asserted it to be hereditary, while others denied it. Colden, in supposing the rank merely a tribute to worth, was in error.

(12) The war chiefs had no rank but what prestige of their own courage and ability gave them.

(13) English and French alike failed in endeavoring to induce them to remove the place of the great council fire.

(14) The Tuscaroras having risen on the people of Carolina in 1710, were finally defeated and retreated north. Lawson, killed in the war, had preserved in his Carolina a vocabulary of the tribe. They settled in New York from 1712 to 1717.

(15) The opening sentence here giving the Iroquois for the name of the league is replaced in the London edition by another falsely charging the Dutch with having preserved nothing relating to the Indians. The name Rodinunchsionni is given as
Hotinnonchiendi

Hotinnonchiendi in the Rel. de la N. F., 1654 (Queb. ed.), p. 11, and there said to mean a complete cabin. This is, doubtless, a Huron form. Bruyas, in his Racines Agnières, gives the name in Mohawk Hotinnonsionni, and it is apparently the third person plural of Gennonsonnisk, "I make a cabin," composed of ganonsa, cabin, and konnis, I make. The modern Mohawk form is Rotinonsionni. Morgan gives the Seneca name as Hodenosaunee, "the people of the long cabin," but this is apparently somewhat free, the term "people" not being in the word. The form Aquanushioni is only a corruption, and the translation "cabin builders" an error arising from ignorance of the Indian thought.

(16) De la Potherie (i. p. 288) took this account, as he did much more of his book, from the manuscript *Moeurs, Couſtumes et Relligion des Sauvages* of Nicholas Perrot, just publiſhed in Paris. (See p. 9 of Tailhan's edition.) Perrot is more explicit than his copiers, and more correct.. "The country of the Irroquois was formerly Montreal and Three Rivers. They had as neighbors the Algonquins dwelling along the Ottawa, at Nipiſſing, French River, and between it and Toronto." Cartier certainly found an Iroquois tribe at Montreal, or Hochelaga. (Hiſt. Mag. ix. 144; Faillon, Hiſtoire de la Colonie Françaiſe i. p. 524.)

(17) The French ſettled at Three Rivers within the remains of a paliſaded (and therefore Huron or Iroquois) town, the charred ends still remaining in the ground, and the cleared fields of the occupants diſcernible. (Rel. 1635, p. 15.)

(18) Perrot does not name Montreal.

(19) Lake Ontario. The French for a time called it Lake Frontenac. Ontara means lake, Ontorio, beautiful lake. Cadarackui, the name here given by Colden to Lake Ontario, was applied by the French to a fort where Kingſton now is, and called alſo Fort Frontenac. Cataraqui is ſaid to mean potter's clay in water.

(20) Corlar's Lake was the old New York name for Lake Champlain, and came from Arendt Van Curler, a Dutch agent high in repute with the Mohawks, who was loſt here, while on his way to Canada on the invitation of the French Governor. The Indians gave his name not only to this Lake but to all Governors at New York.

(21) Champlain's battle with the Mohawks on Lake Champlain was fought in the ſummer of 1609. (See Champlain's account in N. Y. Documentary Hiſtory, iii. 9.)

(22) Colden here omits all account of the war with the Hurons, a more powerful nation than the Adirondacks, and of the ſame race as the Five Nations. They reſided in Upper Canada, near Lake Huron. Joining the Adirondacks, or Algonquins, againſt the Iroquois, they induced Champlain, in 1615, to accompany them on an expedition into Weſtern New York againſt a canton called Entwohonoron, perhaps the Wenro, on whom the Senecas afterwards turned.

(23) Simon Pieſcaret was chief of the " Algonquins

quins of the Ifland," a fmall tribe on the Ottawa, not a general fachem of all the tribes. His courfe might eafily be followed through the French accounts.

(24) This is a very inaccurate fummary; the Iroquois attacked and carried one after another the towns of the Wyandots and Tionontates (Hurons and Petuns) in Upper Canada : and a petty remnant of the former fled to Quebec, and of the latter to Wifconfin. A furprife of a party of the Wyandot refugees on Ifle Orleans in 1657 is the incident referred to by Colden, who overlooks entirely the war in Upper Canada, which fwept away the Wyandot, Tionontate, Attiwandaronk, Wenro and other minor tribes from their ancient feats.

(25) De la Potherie.

(26) De la Potherie, i. 152. The Nepiciriniens, or Nipiffings, never removed to any great diftance. A remnant of the tribe ftill exifts at the Lake of the Two Mountains, and their language for a time prevailed at that miffion.

(27) The Dinondadies fled firft to iflands in Lake Huron, then to the fouthern fhore of Lake Superior, next inland to Black River. Returning then to Mackinaw, they proceeded to Detroit, when a poft was eftablifhed there, and finally croffed to Sandufky, which they named Outfandouke, meaning "There is pure water there." Here they became known to us as Wyandots--the Hurons of Lorette being, however, the original Wyandots. The ifland of the Ottawas is Manitouline, but the name is older than Colden fuppofes. (28)

(28) De la Potherie, i. 303. Piefkaret's death occurred in 1647. (*Relation de la Nouvelle France*, 1647, p. 47.)

(29) There was but one Algonquin village near Quebec, that of Sillery, which eventually filled up with Abnakis, and was removed to St. Francis.

(30) This is the affertion of de la Potherie (ii. 296), but is devoid of all probability or authority.

(31) De la Potherie, ii. 54.

(32) Colden's ignorance as to Arendt Van Curler is ftrange enough. As to him fee O'Callaghan's New Netherland.

(33) De la Potherie, ii. 85. Agariata boafted of having murdered M. de Chazy, the nephew of the Marquis de Tracy. The French Governor was de Courcelle.

(34) The Dutch had one breach with the Mohawks in 1625, when Van Krieekebeck, the Commandant at Albany, joined the Mohegans againft them and was killed.

(35) De la Potherie, Hiftoire de l'Amérique Sept. ii, 87–111. Nicholas Perrot, Moeurs, Couftumes, &c.

(36) 1679.

(37) Lake Erie.

(38) This account of the lofs of the Griffin is from De la Potherie ii. 35-40. (39)

(39) They had been supplied with them nearly fifty years before. *Rel. N. F.* 1643, p. 62.

(40) See New York Colonial Documents III. p. 256, ix. 227.

(41) They were Piscattaways, the Susquehannas had just been conquered by the Iroquois. (See N.Y. Col. Doc. iii. 323, Historical Magazine II. 294.)

(42) New York Colonial Doc. iii. 277. Campbell's Virginia.

(43) These are the Canagesse of p. 31, and the name is preserved under the form of Kanhawa.

(44) Dongan brought out English Jesuits to replace the French, in order to bind the Five Nations to the English interest. (N. Y. Doc. Hist. iii.) The French naturally endeavored to turn the war parties away from themselves.

(45) A treaty between the Five Nations and Maryland in August, 1682, will be found in N.Y. Col. Doc. iii. 321–328.

(46) Assarigoa means Cutlass or Big Knife, and the Dutch word Hower having this signification, the Dutch interpreter gave it as the meaning of Howard! (N. Y. Col. Doc. v. 670.)

(47) An account of the origin of the Laprarie and Caughnawaga missions will be found in a History of the Catholic Missions among the Indian Tribes of the United States, New York, 1855, p. 296.

(48)

(48) Father Lamberville was the only French miſſionary at the time in New York, and that he was able to influence the five different tribes in oppoſition to all the efforts of the authority of New York is not very probable.

(49) Milet was taken priſoner by the Oneidas at Fort Frontenac in 1690, after Denonville entrapped the Iroquois Sachems, and was long in great danger; but his knowledge of the language and long acquaintance with the tribe ſaved him. After he was adopted and regarded as a Sachem, his influence was much dreaded by the Engliſh, and a long correſpondence enſued, his friends ſeeking to prolong his captivity and his enemies to releaſe him. An account of his captivity is printed in the Cramoiſy ſeries. He there ſays that he was adopted as "Otaſſeté, which is the ancient name of one of the firſt founders of the Iroquois Republic," p. 38. Morgan, p. 64, gives as the firſt Oneida Sachem, Hodaſhateh, "a man bearing a burden."

(50) Colden is here in error. A Huron tribe of the town of Scanonaenrat, or St. Michael's, containing many Chriſtians, joined the Senecas, and ſeveral miſſionaries, Garnier, Fremin, Rafeix, Pierron, labored in the Seneca country.

(51) The Sieur de Salvaye. See his Inſtructions in N. Y. Documentary Hiſtory, i. 70.

(52) Charlevoix, Hiſtoire de la Nouvelle France, i. 490, ſays 700 militia, 130 regulars, 200 Indians, chiefly Iroquois of Sault St. Louis, and Hurons or Lorette. The official return of the troops taken at Fort

Fort Frontenac, August 14, 1684, including regulars, militia and Indians, was 34 officers, 782 men. De Meules, the Intendant, says 900 men and 300 Indians.

(53) Supposed to be Salmon river, Oswego county, N. Y. It is said, on p. 79, to be "thirty miles from Onondaga." De la Barre, however, says "four leagues," Charlevoix " four or five leagues from the mouth of their river." i. 493.

(54) Arnold Cornelison Viele was a citizen of Albany and a well known Indian interpreter. For his services in the latter capacity he obtained a grant of land from the Mohawks, September, 1683, a little above Schenectady. The tract was called Wachkeerhoha. (*O'Callaghan.*)

(55) Charles Le Moyne, the founder of one of the illustrious houses of Canada, to which Iberville, Bienville and the Barons Longueuil belonged.

(56) Father John de Lamberville. His Iroquois name of Taorhensere, incorrectly given Twirhaersira on p. 80, means "the man that looks up at the sky." The names given to Missionaries were retained for successors, and the late Mr. Marcoux, missionary at Sault St. Louis, Canada, bore this same name.

(57) Father James de Lamberville.

(58) Called Tegannehout by the French. He was a Seneca ambassador arrested at Quebec by De la Barre. (N. Y. Col. Doc. ix. 239.) He was at the conference at La Famine, or Hungry Bay.

(59) This Indian was not a Sachem. He was merely an orator, and actually in the pay of the French, who called him Grande Gueule. De Meule (Col. Doc. ix. 247) calls him a "sycophant who seeks merely a good dinner and a real buffoon." His real Indian name, as given by the French, was Hotreouati, Hateouati, or Oureouati. La Hontan, or his editor, ignorant of this, and wishing to give his name an Indian turn, transformed Grande Gueule into Grangula, or, as he afterwards wrote it, Garangula. No such Indian name occurs. Morgan, in his list of Onondaga sachem names, gives Hosahaho, Large Mouth, but this differs too much from Hotrewati for us to suppose them identical. Charlevoix, i. 527, strangely confounds him with Tegannehout, the Seneca. De la Barre says that fifteen deputies met him.

(60) La Hontan, i. 48. De la Barre's speech, as originally reported, is in the Documentary History.

(61) This well-known speech, as given here, is taken from La Hontan, Nouveaux Voyages, I. 51–55. The speech of Hotreouati, with the replies of Father Bruyas on behalf of De la Barre, will be found as given by the latter in O'Callaghan's Documentary History, i. 77. La Hontan's is evidently dressed up for his own purposes.

(62) Carachkondie is the Garakontie of the French. The one here alluded to, though confounded by Charlevoix with the great Daniel Garakontie, the far-seeing and enlightened chief of Onondaga, was his brother and successor, and in every way an inferior man. Daniel Garakontie died in 1677. (*Relation*

tion de la Nouvelle France, 1673-9, *Miſſion du Canada*, ii. 202.

(62 *bis*, p. 92) This direct aid to the Iroquois in their attacks on the French poſts, with that afforded them in the maſſacre of the French at Lachine, opened the terrible border wars which form ſuch a bloody page in our Colonial hiſtory. The French, accepting the alternative, welcomed the remnants of the New England Indians, burning with all the ſenſe of wrongs endured, and uſed them ſo effectually that we may well doubt the wiſdom of what Colden here applauds.

(63) The Outagamies are the Foxes, the Kickabous, the Kickapoos: the Maſkoutuh or Maſkutick—properly Maſkoutench, have now diſappeared as a tribe, but were evidently part of or cloſely allied to the Kickapoo nation, into which they ſeem to have been abſorbed. They were all Algonquin tribes, as were the Malhominies and Putewatemies mentioned ſubſequently. The Puans, ſo called from their having come from the ſea, or Fetid Water, are the Winnebagoes, a Dacotah tribe, who ſtyle themſelves Otchagra.

(64) As to the bad faith of the Ottawas on this occaſion, ſee Charlevoix, i. 513.

(65) McGregory's expedition was, under the circumſtances, bold enough, and was baſed on a ſtrange notion of French forbearance. The French officer ſent to arreſt him was Mr. de la Durantaye (Charlevoix, i. 515). For a ſketch of McGregory, who was killed by Leiſler, ſee Col. Doc. iii. 395 *n*.

(66)

(66) The Chief in French interest was Nansouakouet. (De la Potherie, ii. 201.)

(67) This account is from De la Potherie, ii. 203.

(68) De la Potherie, ii. 205. La Hontan, i. 96, ascribes this capture to de Luth.

(69) Charlevoix (vol. i. p. 516) attributes the final action of the Ottawas and Hurons to the influence of Father Anjelran, and says that but for him Michilimackinac would have been in the hands of the English and Iroquois.

(70) Rev. John de Lamberville, S. J. It is extraordinary that Colden omits all mention of the seizure of the chiefs at Fort Frontenac, and of the noble conduct of Garacontie in obtaining for the missionary leave to depart. Charlevoix, i. 504, 510.

(71) By his confession, the English now furnished the Iroquois, their subjects, with material of war to attack the French colonies in the West, after making the furnishing of ammunition to their Indians, by the French, an illegal act. Dongan in fact began war with France.

(72) Colden does not inform us when the English authorities, or the officers sent with the Indian parties, prevented similar acts.

(73) Misprinted Trondequat in the English editions.

(74) For Denonville's expedition see Charlevoix, i. 516; De la Potherie, ii. 207; La Hontan, i. 78;
Col.

Col. Doc., ix. 358-369. The Indian reports to the authorities at Albany are in O'Callaghan's Documentary Hiſtory, i. 151-4. According to O. H. Marſhall, Esq., whoſe inveſtigation of this action is given in the Proceedings of the N. Y. Hiſtorical Society, the battle was fought at Boughton Hill, in the town of Victor, Ontario county, where the railroad croſſes the road. The ſubſequent proceedings of the Onondagas, Cayugas and Oneidas are given in the Col. Doc. ix. 384.

(75) Ohſwego lake is Erie, and Cadarackui Ontario.

(76) The ſeizure of Iroquois chiefs, lured to Fort Frontenac, is one of the moſt ſtriking events of Canadian hiſtory.

(77) The aſſumption of ſovereignty is a ſtep due to Dongan, and the further aſſumption that all territory between the Mohawk and the moſt remote part of an Iroquois raid a conqueſt for England, delightfully abſurd.

(78) The firſt act of hoſtility was the plundering of Frenchmen going to Illinois, a French colony, by men whom Dongan recognized as Engliſh ſubjects.

(79) Liſpenard, whoſe name is ſtill preſerved in one of the ſtreets of New York city, made a report, which is in N. Y. Doc. Hiſtory, i. 155.

(80) The Engliſh occupation of New York being ſo recent, and ſo unjuſt, it is not eaſy to ſee how

the

the Englifh claims could become fuch a gaudy hawk-moth out of the modeft Dutch caterpillar.

(81) It is not eafy to explain who thefe terrible North Indians and Mohegans were, but apparently fome band of Mohegans driven out by the Iroquois and become in French hands a fcourge of the Englifh.

(82) The propofal of Dongan to plant thefe Indians at Saratoga was doubtlefs fincere, though he did not pretend that he would protect them againft their pagan countrymen, whofe violence had driven them into exile. He certainly fent to England for Jefuits to direct them, and we know that Father Charles Gage, Father Thomas Harvey and Father Henry Harrifon actually came to New York for the purpofe. (N. Y. Col. Doc. iii. 73.)

(83) Mifprinted Tames in Englifh editions.

(84) De Nonville does not lofe by comparifon here.

(85) For this account of Adario or Kondiaronk's treachery, fee La Hontan, i. 192. Charlevoix, i. 535, adopts it as true.

(86) La Hontan, i. 193. Charlevoix gives lofs of French at 200. (See De la Potherie, ii. 229.)

(87) For this abandonment of Fort Frontenac fee La Hontan, i. 195, Charlevoix, i. 550. Smith, in his Hiftory of New York, makes it a territorial conqueft of the Mohawks, and confequently of Great Britain!

(88)

Notes.

(88) For Perrot's account of his proceedings, fee Moeurs, Couſtumes et Relligion des Sauvages, Leipſig and Paris, 1864.

www.ingramcontent.com/pod-product-compliance
Lightning Source LLC
Chambersburg PA
CBHW020911230426
43666CB00008B/1416